EMBERS

AN ANGLO-INDIAN MEMOIR

JOY CHASE

DEBEAUX IMPRINT, MENLO PARK, CALIFORNIA

EMBERS: an Anglo-Indian Memoir

Copyright © 2022 Joy Chase

ISBN: 979-8-9863180-0-4

DeBeaux Imprint: Independently published

655 Oak Grove #36, Menlo Park, California 94025, United States of America

Cover photo: The author taken at the bank house in Hyderabad, India in 1961.

Author photo: Taken by Sheila Menezes

A WORD ABOUT THE TYPE

Garamond…font size 12

"…the classic Garamond, named after the type designer Claude Garamond, active in Paris in the first half of the sixteenth century, whose highly legible roman type blew away the heavy fustiness of his German predecessors and later, adapted by William Caslon in England, would provide the letters for the American Declaration of Independence."— Garfield, Simon. Just My Type; a book about fonts. New York: Gotham Books, 2010 p.4.

Headings and titles in Baskerville font, originally designed by John Baskerville in England around 1770.

This book is dedicated
to

My parents: Isabel and Stephen Chase

My daughters: Natala and Sheila Menezes

My siblings:

Margo Heyburn, Jennifer Summerset, Eric Chase

And to
My great aunt: Dr. Esther Chase
My uncle: Leonard Shepherd

ACKNOWLEDGMENTS

I am grateful for
Editors: Naomi Rose and Ruthy Porter
My cousin Greg Bryant for his in-depth genealogical research
Inspiring mentors: Dr. Pamela Eakins & Dr. Paul Augustinovich
Recipe Testers and advisors:
Suvarnamani Divakar Dass, Jean & Joan Wanigasakaran Sheehan,
Shirley Kinoshita, Dawn Podell Driscoll, Meera Lester, Karen Kops.
The Raj Women's group, who have encouraged me throughout this
book's journey and have been meeting for over forty years:
Linda Bruce, Kris Haas, Sue Jackson, Margaret Kuechler,
Mali Mann, Cathy White, Judy William,
and in memory of Elena Venturini Dorabji.

CONTENTS

PART FOUR
THE AFTERMATH AND BEYOND

PART FIVE
END NOTES

PREFACE

I want to make this clear from the outset. I do not accept or condone colonialism. Nor do I have any nostalgia for British Rule in India. As a community, we Anglo-Indians were often put into difficult circumstances depending on acceptance or repudiation by the British who lived and worked in (and colonized) India. Anglo-Indians are the children of so-called mixed marriages between British and Indian during the three-hundred years of occupation. (All in all, the community goes back five hundred years when you include the earlier traders and soldiers who were Portuguese, Dutch and French.) Early on, Anglo-Indians were accepted and promoted but then as the years progressed and Anglo-Indians increased in number, we were not allowed to retain status in the Armed Forces and were relegated to the medical and music sections. Anglo-Indians were almost exclusively put in the communications and transportation services such as the railways, telegraphs, and post offices. They were given these roles mostly after the First War of Independence 1857-59 (also called the Indian or Sepoy Mutiny) in the hope that their British leanings would make them loyal. These jobs were naturally opened up after Independence in 1947 and Anglo-Indians lost their exclusive rights and special privileges. Anglo-Indians tended to adopt British customs and cultural habits primarily because they were not accepted by their Indian counterparts. They had no choice. It was also beneficial to be able to translate and act as a go-between than to be on either side. I remember many Anglo-Indians in pre-and early post-Independence years expressing a hatred for the British in India. The British took on the role of overlords and imposed their laws and religion on the countries of their dominance. They often pretended to higher status than that to which they were born to in England. After many generations in India even the British had a hard time returning to England. They had lost their ability to be the common man having taken on false attitudes of superiority. On the other hand, the Anglo-Indian sometimes showed signs of inferiority while balancing between cultures and creating their own. I believe that it was these very circumstances that allowed Anglo-Indians to rise above the discrimination they had thrown at them both in India and abroad, to value the joie de vivre in hard times and to pass that on to their children. It is this spirit that has enabled Anglo-Indians to thrive worldwide, including in present-day India. My family is just a small sample of this global community.

The invitation from the Queen that my parents received in Bangalore, 1961.

PART ONE
WHAT IT WAS LIKE

1

FIRST THINGS

The Raj had an indescribable quality of survival combined with a dogged determination to enjoy every last good thing; to make all things good things. It was the end of an era. The Raj was slipping away. Indeed, it had gone, but its aura lingered for a while. That strong pioneering spirit and put-up-or-shut-up attitude defined its true identity. Not the political exploitation or colonial mores that dim it now.

Although it has been many years since I resided in India, I still have vivid recollections of that abundant, humble, and unique way of life that the Anglo-Indian lived and epitomized. What was known as the Raj Era, or the Colonial Era, ended with India's Independence in 1947. In the days of the family meal, my mother and my grandmothers filled our collective memories with the vivid tastes, sounds and smells of India whose salient parts I record here. After my mother and father eventually migrated to Australia, Dad made the best fish curry, based on his memories of his mother, Adelaide, cooking in her small kitchen when he was a boy. The heady aroma of fish frying in a pan with very little oil—be it pomfret, seer or just a few fresh sardines—brings back memories both ancient and primal.

My mother, Isabel, with me as a baby in 1941.

Sometimes the stories of India create the impression that Anglo-Indians were rich and lived a grand lifestyle. Although that might seem to be the case, compared to what is available and affordable today, it wasn't like that. Labor was bountiful and respected. This made it possible for a woman of the Raj to organize and supervise a large household staff, or, at the least, one errand boy and odd job wallah. (A wallah, is a Hindi-derived word sometimes associated with a specific task or profession.) Due to the unaccustomed heat (in some places) and the lack of water and other amenities, housework in India in the early days was too difficult for women who came from England.

Nevertheless, it was certainly more attractive, than scrubbing pots or floors in dreary England. Life must be lived wherever you are, and the Anglo-Indians lived it to the best of their ability at the time and in the place where they were, as they do to this day in their new and adopted countries.

I want to tell you more about me and my ancestors. I was born in Coimbatore in 1940 and raised in India. My parents, Isabel (Shepherd) Chase and Stephen Chase, were born in India and lived there most of their lives, staying on past the diaspora of the Anglo-Indian community. They emigrated to Australia in 1967. My mother was born February 7, 1921, at the Garrison hospital in Wellington in the Nilgiris in South India. She was baptized at St. George's Church in Wellington. At that time her father, Harry (Henry James) Shepherd was a Staff Sergeant in the 20th Nilgiris and Malabar Battalions in the Auxiliary Force in India.

On my maternal side, my grandmother, (my mother's mother) Florence (Florrie) Grace Lillywhite was born in Bangalore on September 19, 1871 and baptized in Toomkoor or Tumor near Nagpur. She lived in India and migrated to England soon after Independence, but later returned to India disillusioned. She eventually returned to England where she died in 1959. My great grandmother, Florence Lilian Clapham (known as Lilly, sometimes nicknamed Joy) was born in India and lived there her entire life. She was buried at the Hosur cemetery in Bangalore in 1946, a year before Indian Independence. She would have many stories to tell.

My great-great grandmother, Jane Harriet De Beaux, was born in India and married my great-great grandfather Mathew Clapham III in 1865 at the then largest church in Asia, St. Andrew's also known as the Scott's Kirk in Madras. Mathew Clapham became inspector of schools in Bangalore and died in 1908 at almost seventy years of age. At the end of his life, he was a government pensioner living in Nimar, an area now known as Khargone in Madhya Pradesh.

My grandmother Florence, my grandfather Harry, and their son
Harry Roslyn Haig, 1919.

Jane Harriet's father Benjamin Louis Joseph De Beaux was born in Bangalore in 1819. Her grandfather, also Benjamin Louis De Beaux, was probably born in Madras or Bangalore, as were her grandmothers. He was married in Arcot, Madras in 1817. Seven generations before me were born in India. We are Indian by birthright and Anglo-Indian by culture.

My grandfather, Harry Shepherd, was English, from Norwich in Norfolk. My grandmother, who had nine children, did not want to go back to England with him, although they eventually did. India was her home. India is still our home. Wherever Anglo-Indians live, all over the world, they will tell you that India is their home and the country where they live—which may be home to their children or grandchildren—is simply the country of domicile. I feel comfortable in my skin in India where I feel that I belong.

George Honey, my first ancestor from Britain on my mother's side came out to India in 1830 on the good ship Minerva and married Charlotte Young, an Indo-Britain whose family had been in India for generations. The De Beaux family had been in India for a few generations before George Honey arrived. The female line has yet to be researched and documented. It is buried under the stones of India.

My dad, Stephen Joseph William Chase, was born in 1908 in Katpadi in Madras State now Tamilnadu, the land of the Tamils. My father's family lived in Madras not far from Fort St. George. They are inter-married and intra-married and did not leave India until the nineteen sixties, and, even now, many have not.

My grandfather, Harry Shepherd with medals he won during the Wars.

I remember taking a long green chili fresh off a bush by the kitchen and relishing it's fresh and fiery flavor. I remember the delight of fish frying with turmeric and cumin wafting from the kitchen, and Alice, our one time cook, making my favorite birthday meal of meat-stuffed snake-coys (a long zucchini-like vegetable), smooth dal, and fluffy papadums (crispy chips) with their crackling, and a little spoonful of my mother's hot, sweet mango chutney. Sunday afternoons, after church, coming home to Yellow Rice and Chicken Curry with fresh tomato, onions, and yogurt to cool the heat of the warm cardamom, cloves, and cinnamon. Those were the days past the Raj, and for a while it was still the Raj life. We can take that concept of the Raj life into the present to taste and feel the essence of that time without the resentment and bitterness of the colonial era.

The Scott's Kirk, St. Andrews in Madras/Chennai. Photo by me.

When Anglo-Indians left India, they took with them a cooking tradition of aromatic curries, flavorful soups, and exotic meat dishes. It is a rich mixture of an English diet intertwined with Indian spices and sauces cooked in a particular way associated only with our community in India. They borrowed from both Indian and British freely to create a cuisine they called their own. They threw in a little Portuguese, Dutch, Danish and French.

I've decided to write down my memories because I believe I am unique. I believe each of us is unique. Every day of my life, and of each person's life, is unique and different from everyone else's. I will share with you my life as I record some snippets, some moments, a memory here and there. Perhaps time has rendered them with an added glow, but they are still mine—still unique. I also give thanks for my life and my health, and I want to share what I can of the blessings with you.

There are aspects of my life as an Anglo-Indian growing up in India that are also common experiences to many Anglo-Indians who come from my community and I hope to capture some of our collective culture, too.

2

COBRAS, SCORPIONS, CROWS, TIGERS, AND OTHERS

COBRAS

There will always be snakes in India. Six-foot-long snakes lived in the tall grass by the back shed of our house in Madras, creating waves in the grass as they slithered around. My father did not have the gardener cut down the grass, probably because he was afraid to rustle up the snakes. These snakes were not poisonous, so it was good to leave them alone.

There were (and still are) very poisonous snakes in India. My mother often told of the time when we were living in Telicherry (famous for its peppercorns). I was three and she walked into the living room to find a beautiful glistening cobra curled up asleep on the couch —and little me standing there mesmerized. It was a king cobra, with a wide, threatening hood and a forked tongue darting quickly in and out of its cup-shaped mouth. In and out went his forked tongue. When he was awake, his big eyes went around and around on his head. My mother was shocked and surprised but managed to pick me up quickly and quietly and get us out of the room. She then ran to find the mali (our gardener), to take care of the snake. This was no small task. He had to pass the word along to get the local snake charmer, with his special flute (that looked more like a bugle) recognized throughout India for its deep haunting melodies that charm snakes. The sound drew your spirit and enveloped your senses till you, too, felt like following the king cobra. The mali brought the snake charmer to our house to play those haunting flute melodies until the cobra followed him out to the fields and slithered away into his hole.

After that day of the king cobra visit, we always kept snakebite remedies in the house. During all my years in India, Dad would call us together and show us where he kept the snakebite antidote and teach us repeatedly how to use it if we got bitten. He warned us to "keep walking" and to not let the poison take over our bodies. We were taught to mix the white crystals with the black crystals and add potassium permanganate in water to create a snake-bite antidote. We learned how to place a tourniquet to keep the venom from traveling throughout the body, and to keep the person who had been bitten awake and walking. This experience was quite different from the casual occurrence of seeing a snake charmer in the bazaar, with his cobra tucked well into its snake basket. When this snake fanned out its hood and flickered its forked tongue, we were reassured that its venomous bite had been removed by some secret procedure known only to the snake charmer.

We often saw snake charmers in the bazaars with their baskets of snakes, their bugles and crowds gathered around. Those markets were filled with people intent on buying produce of every exotic variety: mangoes, bananas, and cashew nuts, or sometimes a squawking chicken. While standing in a clearing at the market my dad told me he had actually seen the rope trick performed when he was a boy. A fakir conjured a crowd and made a rope slowly emerge from a basket, like a snake; but it rose straight up in the air and was climbed by a young boy accomplice. In India, stories of this magic trick have been told all the way back to the ninth century. It is no longer performed these days, possibly because the cities have become so busy that there is neither a clearing nor a willing belief in this wonderful magic anymore.

There are fewer snakes now, but we had a cook in Bangalore who was very brave. He encountered a viper on his way from the kitchen to the house and killed it by stamping on it with his bare feet. My mother remembers a time my father killed a snake, too.

Rudyard Kipling wrote about Rikki-Tikki-Tavi, the good mongoose. But the mongoose I saw in the corner of the living room scared me so much that I screamed and screamed! My dad came in and asked me what I had seen. "This big furry thing as large as a dog!" I said. Dad was quite delighted. He explained to me that it was a good sign because I had just seen a mongoose. Its hair was puffed up because it felt threatened and was trying to frighten me away. A mongoose was a good sign because they kill snakes. At that time, cobras were living in the acreage around our house, so seeing a mongoose was truly a good thing.

My dad had many practical aspects to his knowledge, some of which he learned as an Eagle Scout in his youth. He would tell us that as a scout he once shook the hand of the scout who shook the hand of the future king of England when he visited India. The Indian Boy Scouts Association was founded in India in 1916.

My father went to considerable expense to have small broken granite pieces laid in a three-foot strip all around the house to protect us from snakes trying to enter the house. The snakes would not cross this sharp, rough barrier.

The prevailing theory, in India, was that you do not go out and slaughter the snakes like in the Irish legend of St. Patrick. It was believed that if you killed a snake the mate would lie in wait to kill you, so you would gain nothing. Chuchundra, the muskrat in Kipling's Jungle Book said, "Those who kill snakes get killed by snakes." In the urban area that surrounded this particular house in Madras, there was no snake charmer or a snake hostel to send the snakes. Keeping the brush down, if you could hire someone to do this, and creating boundaries that snakes would not cross, was all that could be done.

This was the house, "Red Craig" in Madras/Chennai where my father installed a granite border. Photo taken by me in 1984. View from the front.

Rudyard Kipling described Rikki-Tikki-Tavi, like the mongoose I saw that night:

> He was a mongoose, rather like a little cat in his fur and his tail, but quite like a weasel in his head and his habits. His eyes and the end of his restless nose were pink; he could scratch himself anywhere he pleased, with any leg, front or back, that he chose to use; he could fluff up his tail till it looked like a bottle-brush, and his war-cry, as he scuttled through the long grass, was: "Rikk-tikk-tikki-tikki-tchk!"

SCORPIONS

My mother told me of a huge black scorpion that she found in her bed when she was a child—it was about three inches long and furry. Despite their deadly sting, scorpions co-existed with humans. Once when I pulled my chair out to sit down for dinner at a friend's home in Madras, a scorpion fell to the floor, its wicked tail curving up. Quickly, I stepped on it, extinguishing its life before it could move. Luckily, I had my shoes on. We never knew when a scorpion would decide to enter a house. The common scorpions in Madras were brown and only about an inch long. We lived in the warm, humid tropics and took its flora, fauna and active animal and insect life in stride. To this day I have a quick kill-or-be-killed attitude toward biting bugs, unlike some people who like to coerce them onto pieces of newspaper and deposit them in the great outdoors. My dad said there were two kinds of people: the quick and the dead. When it comes to scorpions—I am quick!

The iceman delivered ice from the ice factory in Madras. The factory is now a museum to the memory of Vivekananda, a sage who visited America in 1893 and died in 1902. Originally, ice was shipped from Newfoundland to India, but in later years it was made on site. The ice, covered in sawdust, was placed in our icebox where it would last about a week before having to be replaced. The ice was delivered by bullock cart, as was the straw for the cows. We would sit in the dining room, the icebox in the corner keeping the milk cool.

One day, my sister and I were drinking our cooled milk when our ayah (children's maid), Muni-ma, grabbed the cup from my sister's mouth and threw the milk on the ground outside the door. We were shocked and started screaming for our mother who came running, as did Alice, our cook, who came from the outside kitchen. An ugly scorpion crawled away into some leftover bricks from the construction of a pen for our egg-laying English Leghorn hens. My sister's life had just been saved by Muni-ma.

Although the Raj Life with ayahs and cooks seems special, it was normal for the times. Even then, my mother told me that they couldn't afford a dining table, so they made one by screwing together four large deal-wood boxes and covering them with a tablecloth. Deal wood was like pine wood, soft and easy to saw. Our apartment then was one quarter of a house, but its two-story high Asoka tree made us feel grand. My dad remembered that his family had many deprivations when he was young. He would bring home his check from his job as a clerk in the bank and give it to his brother, Richard, who managed the household for their widowed mother. One time, when he could not afford the one anna he needed to buy a stamp, he walked all the way home from work to save that one anna instead of taking the bus.

CROWS

Crows and ravens in India are seldom mentioned, and yet they are pervasive. I was so annoyed, at around age eleven, when reading The Secret Garden, by Frances Hodgson Burnett, that the main character had supposedly never seen a crow, although she had lived in India. I knew this was impossible, so I closed the book and did not read it until much later in life.

My dad Stephen Joseph William Chase (1908-1993) in the 1940s

Crows used to circle the house by the hundreds whenever a crow was killed or died. We called it a "crow funeral." Round and round they would go, sometimes for hours. Then, one or two at a time, they would make speeches from our rooftop.

Crows were grey and black and smaller than the ravens. Ravens were larger and all black with very bright eyes and beaks. My dad used to have a catapult (called a catty) which he made himself from a Y-shaped twig and a strip of rubber from an old tire. These were tied together with string and the whole thing would fit in his hand. He would make half-inch round catty balls from mud and dry them slowly in the sun. This was only when there seemed to be too many crows stealing food. One day, he would pick up his catty, pull back the rubber band with a mud ball in position and shoot at the birds until he killed one. Then he would cut off a wing and hang it on the back door after he had buried the rest of the bird's body. The crows would have their funeral and then move on, for a while.

Crows were large scary birds, especially for a child. Once, when I was about ten, I was eating a sandwich on the steps at Doveton-Corries School in Madras when a huge crow swooped down and snatched it out of my hand, ripping my fingers as it left. They were very bold. These steps were on the side of the main building by a big open shed where we used to play out of the sun. We used to knock ripe tamarinds out of the enormous tamarind tree to suck on. They were delicious and sour. This tree has been cut down and the students are dependent on the vendors by the gates for ripe tamarinds or green mangoes with chili powder.

When I was fourteen and away at boarding school in Ooty, I was chased by some boys who had a dead crow they had found. I fell on some brambly bushes and got a big thorn in my palm. I had to go to Emergency to have it removed. I had a lump in my palm for years. Not satisfied with having chased me with a dead crow, these boys continued to tease me and gave me some version of the word "crow" as a nickname. Crows. I liked the ravens a lot more—they seemed to have a mystical side to their personalities, so black and shiny with their bright eyes.

TIGERS

If we were in Madras, my dad would get the idea to visit Tiger Green, who's real first name was Russel. He was a friend of my dad's for many, many years. We would all pile into our Ford V8 car and drive out past what was then the edge of town to where Tiger Green and his family lived. There we would spend the day, my parents in animated conversation with Tiger, his wife and assorted dependent aunts or sisters. We children roamed the garden, climbed trees, and played traditional outdoor games like seven tiles, hopscotch or hide and seek. Tiger's walls were covered with the skins of tigers he'd shot, with their heads stuffed so that they seemed alive. There were skins on the walls as well as on the floor. Over the doors were stuffed heads with huge horns—a nilgai or a stag. His coffee table was an old shiny brass tray, about 3-4 feet across. It was low to the ground, perched on a branched rosewood stand. On top of the table were numerous brass animals of all shapes and forms—tigers, leopards, lizards, crocodiles, dogs, and birds. There were also cabinets filled with china and crystal, but I was not interested in those. The room was darkened with curtains on every side to keep out the ever-bright sunshine, although all the doors were open and the ubiquitous electric ceiling fans whirled on and on. Tea was served.

Tiger Green had a pet monkey tied to a tree with plenty of rope, whose teeth marks still adorn my wrist. While Dad discussed the latest tiger hunt with Tiger inside the house, my sisters and I investigated the garden. We got too close to the monkey, and he wanted my little red purse, which I happened to be swinging in his face. I got more than I bargained for when he proceeded to jump on my head. I waved my arms wildly to dislodge him, which earned me the trophy monkey bite. My screams brought everyone out of the house. I was then subjected to the ritual of pouring iodine on my wound, soliciting more screams but cauterizing the bite. I was then trucked off to the doctor, where I was duly bandaged and extolled to never tease a monkey again. The big question was, did the monkey, pet or not, have rabies? He was kept under observation for ten days and I was, too. Fortunately, the monkey was just fine, and I avoided the ten shots in the stomach for rabies, which was the preventative medicine of the time. And the pet monkey avoided being put to death to prevent the spread of rabies.

While tigers have taken on a mythological quality in India and in most of the world, fifty or a hundred years ago they were a very real threat, terrifying villages when they became man-eaters. Tiger Green only killed man-eaters. A tiger that was lame or hungry during a drought would sometimes taste human blood, find it good and an easy prey and then satisfy his/her hunger by preying on stray village folk. Many famous tiger hunts ensued. Although there were trophy tiger hunts (in which tigers were hunted practically into extinction by Indian princes and Englishmen alike), the tiger hunts to save the lives of people were most admired and necessary. Tiger Green was often called upon to perform this important task.

It was Tiger Green who I thought of years later in America when I was asked if I had ever had tiger's milk to drink. There was a brand of dried or condensed milk in India that I barely remembered, but quick to the draw, my imagination gone wild, I said "Yes! In fact, (I elaborated) in India we had tiger farms where we kept tigers in stalls and milked them with electric milking machines like the tame cows in Wisconsin." (Yes, sure.)

My friend Wendy, the Soura tribal girl from Orissa (now Odisha), was certainly not thinking of milking a tiger the week a tiger came to visit where she lived with her adoptive mother, the missionary Catherine Munro, way out in the country. Wendy was the first of many children that Miss Munro adopted. There was nothing Miss Munro could do when the tiger came to visit. He just walked into the compound and climbed up into a tree right next to the entrance to their house. This tiger wasn't a little cat that you could call the fire department to bring meowing down. This was a big 300-pound, snarling, growling tiger with all its stripes. They just stayed in the house, peaking out now and then through a tightly shut window until, several days later, the tiger decided he'd had enough, climbed down and just walked away. How I wished I had lived out in the country to witness these sights myself, although it was terrifying to Wendy and her mother, stuck in their house for days. The tree forever smelled of tiger and no mere kitty would ever voluntarily climb it. I had to console myself with the sounds of lions roaring early in the morning from the Madras Zoo.

Before the cities and towns grew and became a magnet for people leaving the villages, Lady Curzon, wife of Viceroy Lord Curzon, wrote in her diary that a large Bengal tiger often came to the back door of the Viceroy's palace in Calcutta to take a few licks of the milk that was waiting to be served for breakfast.

When I was in boarding school in the hills, we would go camping during short holidays when it was not practical to fly back home to Sri Lanka in the hot summer. Setting up camp in the outskirts of Ooty, it was fun to be the advance guard. Jackals howled the first night and we dug ditches all around the tents to channel the heavy monsoon rain. Whitened carcasses of buffalo, eaten by a tiger, lay nearby. Four of us went up from the base camp for an additional eight-mile hike higher in the hills, through the mists above a village called Bangitapal. We stopped by a crystal-clear stream that had been planted with large trout. Our leader and the other member of the team hiked on, but soon returned. They had seen three tiger cubs in a clearing of the mist

—but not the tigress. Not wishing to confront her by accident, they made a quick retreat. I missed seeing those little tiger cubs. But taking a walk with another friend, beating our way through the four-foot-high grasses, we heard grunts above us. As we kept going, we then heard grunts below. Again, we made a quick retreat and missed seeing a tiger. Tigers don't attack humans unless the tiger is a man-eater.

We went on an elephant ride through the preserve jungle. The grass reached above the elephant's knees. We swayed side to side as he waddled through the grass, grabbing some sweet branches, and wading through streams. Although we hoped to see a tiger, we only saw the wild nilgai and a stag with tall branching antlers staring straight at us, as bizarre as we looked up there on the elephant.

We drove up the ghats with a driver for a reunion at our school in Ooty. Chatting along we went when the driver suddenly slowed and then stopped the car telling us to be quiet. "Yani, yani" he said, in Tamil. I knew he had spotted an elephant in the wild, a precious gift on this trip. We looked and there she was, magnificent, larger than our car, with a lovely baby elephant trailing her. Never forget!

A photo of me at the Mudumalai Wildlife Sanctuary est. 1940.

Poems from the nineteenth century British poets that we memorized in grade school, even in India, often come back to light up my mind's eye. My dad often quoted a poem he had to memorize as a boy, *The Tyger*, by William Blake who was born on my birthday in 1757. He repeated this verse in his poem like a chorus:

Tyger, tyger, burning bright
In the forests of the night,
What immortal hand or eye
Could frame thy fearful symmetry?

OTHER TROPICAL CREATURES

My dad had a Daisy gun with which my sister was a crack shot. She would pick that thing up and aim it once and down would come her target! When we lived on Spur Tank Road, in Madras, large flying foxes would swing across the Cooum River from the big trees on the other side but it was when we lived in Bangalore that my sister practiced her best marksmanship. We lived upstairs in a house with a very high ceiling, and the bats would accidentally get trapped inside the house and circle, afraid to swoop down towards the doors while they picked up sonic radar from our erratic movements below. Margo would lift the Daisy and bring the poor bat down with one shot. "Bravo!" I would say softly, while hiding under the mosquito net on my bed. Eventually, we learned that if we sat still, the bat would keep circling lower and lower until it found the large open doors and fly out. Years later, my friend encountered a similar situation in Venezuela when a bat had become trapped inside her house up on a hill. She called me in America, and I told her to just sit still. Poor bats, they are so maligned.

I actually preferred the monkeys to the bats. They came through the open windows to steal a banana or a mango. Monkeys seemed more human. Once much later, when my daughter made a face at a monkey in India, the monkey made a face back. There used to be a lot more monkeys in Bangalore but there are still a few around.

Tigers, cobras, bats, and scorpions thrive in the lush tropical climate and are battled daily. Soon after I left India, I was invited to camp out at a stuga (cottage) in Minnesota, with some good friends. Not having been taught to cook or clean much in India, I was not much use. Even my style of making tea was considered odd, as I refused to stew the tea leaves in the Swedish way. But when a dead rat was found rolled into a sofa bed, I rose to the challenge. Dead rats were not to be feared in India, live rats were much worse. Nonchalantly, I picked the deceased rodent up by its tail and tossed it outside without a qualm. Thereafter, I was considered a qualified camper in their eyes.

If they only understood what I knew about the tropics! Encounters with bats, rats, scorpions, tree ants, cockroaches, kumbli boochees, bundoos and centipedes were common. Mr. Allaby, a missionary in Orissa, had clocked a cheetah in his jeep running at 35 mph but they can run much faster than that. The centipedes often had orange spots on them. Kumbli boochees were cute little hairy caterpillars that curled up into a blanket-like ball when you picked them up. (A boochee is an insect or caterpillar and kumbli means blanket in Tamil.) Bundoos were all the rest of the cute little bugs—the ones that did not bite. Bundoo was a term of endearment, in fact, and I often called my children little bundoos as they were growing up. Kutti, meaning little, was another term of endearment in Tamil. I named my cute little cockapoo dog Kutti Appa Gramani after a street in Madras where my aunt and uncle lived. We just called him Kutti (little).

I went to Doveton-Corries Girls School in Madras when its vast fields were still undeveloped. We could play out of the sun in a pavilion or in the open fields. Sometimes we would draw hopscotches with chalk on the hard surface of the outdoor netball court. We called it butch and played with stones. Beyond this space, and further than the enormous tamarind tree, was a shady area with tall grass and a stream. There we would search for gold bees, large, beautiful bugs with shiny green, red, or gold wings. We would catch a couple, put them in shoeboxes with some grass, and take them home to enjoy for a while. They were beautiful creatures, a kind of golden tortoise beetle. (Now gold bees refer to gold investments on the stock exchange.)

Doveton-Corrie's School front and back. Motto: Play the Game.

Sitting outside was a respite from the heat late in the evenings. Fireflies by the dozen lit up the sky. During the day, dragonflies swarmed over the grass. My dad showed us how to stalk them by getting a reed, tying a long hair to it (often my mother's) and fixing a small ball of wax to the end. Then we would stand quietly until we caught a dragonfly and put it in a jar. (Although dragonflies diminished in those days, I was happy to hear that they have been rediscovered after 87 years.)

Exotic butterflies were everywhere, especially in the hills. The Russian American writer Vladimir Nabokov, with his butterfly obsession, would have been delighted. Large butterfly nets were common, catching many different species until sadly, many became extinct. The richness of the jungle overflowed to the cities. Fortunately, there is a resurgence of butterflies, too. To live in India during this time was to experience the tropics in their entire splendor and darkness.

3
THE PRESIDENCIES

The British divided India into three Presidencies to make this large, complex country simpler to govern and administer and thus better serve their own needs. The division, as elsewhere in the British Empire such as in Africa, was arbitrary and did not adhere to local custom, or even language and cultural differences. These three Presidencies were: (changes occurred over time)

Bombay, which covered the west and north of the country, including what is now Pakistan.

Bengal, which covered the east of the country and included Burma and what is now Bangladesh.

Madras, which covered the southern portion of India. At one time "Madras" included Singapore, and Burma, but not Ceylon (Sri Lanka), which was considered a Crown Colony and governed directly from London.

The main cities of the Presidencies were Bombay (Mumbai),

Calcutta (Kolkata) and Madras (Chennai), respectively. It was through the Anglican churches in these Presidency capitals that the records of birth, marriage, and death (BMD) of British and Anglo-Indian people were sent to India House in London. They were consequently deposited at the British Library, where they can be found and researched today.

Research can be conducted about the Presidencies on the Internet. As time went by, changes were made to these territories. I recommend this FIBIS page https://wiki.fibis.org/w/Presidencies for maps and more detail. The Families in British India Society (FIBIS) is a self-help organization devoted to members researching their British India family history and the background against which their ancestors led their lives in India under British rule.

BOMBAY THE FORMER PRESIDENCY

Bombay (Mumbai) its major city, was acquired from Portugal in 1661. You can feel the gentle sea breezes off the ocean, with no one around in the early morning. Skies sparkle through that magnificent 'Gateway to India', which still imposes its presence on Bombay. Standing here you get the full, heady treat that is this city. The mythic Elephanta caves are a mere boat ride away. Ignorant British Tommies (soldiers) and earlier vandals had used the ancient carvings for target practice, leaving their ugly marks behind. The ocean, like translucent silk, winds itself back and forth from the Taj Hotel to the islands. The Taj itself evokes another time, another place, as it rises from the maelstrom of traffic, vendors multiplied by population increases and visitors morphed into tourists, welcoming guests in a maintained splendor uniquely its own. The Taj hotel gives a nod to times long gone. The Palm restaurant offers sofas and settees with an unparalleled view of Bombay. Sit and enjoy tea for two or three hours, no less. The silver tea sets on trays, club soda, bel puris (nowadays) and all things lovely (and maybe rare) are available here—for a price. People-watching in the lobby, on the veranda, or up the branching wrought iron grand staircase with its filigree banisters is a lovely pastime. The Raj life is alive today at the Taj in a very Indian way.

Bombay is the most intricate of cities, neighborhoods within neighborhoods bordering on other neighborhoods—Christian, Muslim and Anglo-Indian. Even its residents may never see all of it. Now, with the addition of high pass-overs and bridges and tiered highways crushing and slicing the city into pieces, one can peer over the edges into areas one could never visit—a mosque here, with its markets and wares; a temple there, with hordes of devoted people pressing up to its doors carrying coconuts and bright orange flowers; a church, the uplifting Gloria, six stories tall, rising from the ground in the shadow of the oldest mosque's call to prayer. Except for brief interludes of strife, they all live together peacefully—Jews, Parsis (who were originally from Persia), Catholics and Muslims with Hindus and Sikhs. This is, and has always been, Bombay. As the song goes, mere Bombay. My Bombay.

Mumba Devi, the patron goddess of the koli fisher folk, who are its oldest inhabitants, has reclaimed Bombay, (now called Mumbai). The monsoon thrashes it severely each year. The storied four million people who live in the streets and the train stations are very present. The tiffin-carrier organization that brings everyone their lunch is efficient. The still beautiful Victoria Station—in that Indo-Saracen style made popular in the early 1900s by architects Wittet and Heiton —welcomes the millions who ride the Bombay trains, even now, every day.

My great-grandfather, Patrick Lilywhite, lived and later died in Bombay, and many of my mother's Lilywhite cousins still live in Mumbai and its outskirts. The city now has twenty-million residents. A trip down to the Colaba Causeway (known as Shahid Bhagat Singh Road officially now) with its embarrassment of riches, forces you to purchase things you will never use although you bargained earnestly, and enough Bombay halva for twelve days.

My great-grandfather, Patrick Lilywhite. (Photo: My Heritage)

BENGAL NOW IN BANGLADESH AND WEST BENGAL

Calcutta (Kolkata) is a major city and the capital of West Bengal. Job Charnock, of the East India Company, is credited with having founded Calcutta, now Kolkata, in 1690. Excavations indicate that an ancient civilization flourished in this region long before that. A grand city, with its shining silver suspension bridge, the Howrah Bridge, over the Hooghly River, it was the capital of India (for the British) for a time. Howrah Bridge, which connects the smaller city of Howrah to Calcutta was renamed in 1965 to honor the poet Rabindranath Tagore but it is still called the Howrah Bridge colloquially. The Victoria Memorial Museum is impressive, with its sixteen-foot statue of the Angel of Victory on top, its lawns and bright white marble buildings glowing under the bright sun. And yet, with its huge population, I would watch from a window when we lived there, the dead coming out the back doors of the hospitals, their male relatives, chanting "Ho Gaya, ho gaya," He's gone, he's gone. This was the underbelly of a great city. The enormous annual parade of Kali is a procession to the riverbed. As children, we were not allowed to eat the shish kebabs sold on the streets, but my parents ate them in secret because they tasted so good. There were crowds, always crowds. The large Chinese settlement and the Armenian Community in Calcutta lived alongside Anglo-Indians.

I attended Pratt Memorial School for Girls in Calcutta for a year while we lived there. The buses were loaded with people inside and out, hanging on. A male employee always accompanied us, pushing us inside and hanging on to the outside all the way to Pratt. Then he calmly escorted us—in our slightly mussed uniforms—into the private school where we spent the day protected by its tall walls. Meanwhile, he braved the bus to return home, only to come out again to pick us up at the end of the school day. We studied Bengali, with its aspirated alphabet. My mother had a book with pictures and English pronunciations. Kela and Khela were similar words. She did her best and asked the cook to buy a hundred pounds of Khela, which she had determined meant coal, that we used for all our cooking needs. The cook returned with a huge stalk of bananas—one hundred pounds! We waited for some to ripen, baked some with coconut, put them in custard puddings, mashed them up with cream and sugar and, of course, shared them. Bananas instead of coal—words that were one aspirant apart.

Calcutta incorporated high style, next to hovels of poverty. Thousands of refugees slept in the streets, and many years later, Mother Teresa and some local organizations redeemed some of them by their work among the poorest of the poor. New Market originally a Victorian Gothic designed bazaar was filled with shops, a lane for each kind of product; shoes down this one, toys down that, rolls of material, pots and pans, flowers. I loved the flower aisle, with its heady fragrance of jasmine and lilies, sweet and honey-like. The blossoms were large and small, and the colors spanned the

My mother, Isabel, in her sharkskin dress circa 1951.

rainbow, from orange and red to white and ivory. Transfixed, I wandered away from my family. My mother's mind skipped to stories about stolen girls, underground prostitution rings, forced belly dancing and such. I was lost but not yet unhappy, neither stolen nor sad but just a little bit afraid. I heard my father's distinctive whistle, a roll and a lilt that we had come to recognize as the family call. I followed it past the shoes, past the pots and pans, and past the toys until our family was reunited and I was berated for wandering off. No public hugs and kisses in New Market. With a silent bravado, I took it in stride and imagined a self-hug that day.

MADRAS NOW TAMILNADU, PREVIOUSLY ALSO INCLUDED ANDHRA

Madras (Chennai) is the capital and largest city in Tamilnadu. Chennai is on the Coromandel Coast in the Bay of Bengal. The name, Madras, came from the site of the village Madras Patnam settled in 1639 by the British, where a Fort named for St. George was established. The city was founded by Mr. Francis Day. Many of my ancestors, on both my father's and my mother's sides, come from Madras. The village of Chennai pre-dates British rule, and after many years was able to reestablish its dominance over the villages that grew together in this area. People tell of the rice flats and bunds that existed before the roads and houses were built. Even the long Mount Road was built on an original cart track which went back centuries.

The Chases have a long history in this south Indian city. My dad attended Christ Church school as a boy. He had a love for their church steeple and often took me (when it was still accessible in the late 1940s) to climb it with him and view the whole city of Madras back then.

He then went on to finish school at Bishop Corrie's High School. As an adult my dad sent a gift of a carved silver betel nut box for his math teacher to thank him for teaching him mathematics and tell him how he valued what he had learned in his job as a high-ranking banker. The teacher was so moved that he was brought to tears. Betel nuts are the seeds of the areca palm which are often chewed for their caffeine-like qualities and medicinal value.

Corrie's school was joined with Doveton although it continued as a school. I went to the girl's school of Doveton-Corrie. My cheeks felt warm with pride when I was the Queen of Hearts in the school play on Prize Day. I felt the fluttering of my heart when I played the part of St. George, who slew the dragon. The boys got to shake hands, but the girls had to curtsey when we received prizes. We practiced that curtsey until we got it just right. But this is my city.

*My dad Stephen with his parents, Albert and Adelaide, his sister
Eunice, and his older brother Richard taken in 1920.*

After World War II, pilots of small planes flew low, flew high, and
did dangerous somersaults in the sky—my beautiful aunts Gwen and
Doris (Honie) and me—while we walked on the broad, open sand at
Eliot's Beach in Madras we watched them, and they noticed us. The
fish sparkled in the water after dark. Pretty shells and jellyfish lying on
the beach belied the fact that there had been a war. Everyone we knew
seemed to have left or was leaving India. Not quite everyone, but
almost, it seemed.

Christ Church and school in Madras.

The trams ran up Poonamalee High Road, but soon became too expensive and the unions too strong. Eventually they were discontinued, and the tracks dug up. I rode the trams for half an anna, a square coin that has also gone the way of history. Many beautiful buildings along that route have all gone—the Moor Markets, the Ripon Buildings—but the grand Central Railway station still thrives and even sells tickets online.

Madras is the city I lived longest in, and it has the greatest pull and deepest memories for me. I feel the heady spices, nicely melded into the flavorful dishes that my grandmother used to make. Despite the hurry burry of the traffic and the population exponentially greater than when I was a resident, I still feel a deep peace and have happy bubbles in my heart when I am in Madras. It has been our hometown for generations.

My sister Margo shared research she had done on the Chase lineage, William Chase was a linen draper in Cornell, England around 1690. His son Richard Chase lived in Kensington around 1720, having done quite well. His son, also Richard Chase was a Lieutenant in the British Army in India. He was born in 1753 and died in 1834. He was Mayor of Pondicherry and an Alderman and briefly Mayor of Madras, too, in 1800. He was also a prisoner of Tippu Sultan in

Mysore. His son Stephen Chase was born in 1822 and later became a minister at the London Mission Church in Madras. My great-grandfather, Benjamin Chase (1838), my grandfather Albert Chase (1867) and my uncle Richard all were from Madras.

Parry's Corner in Madras in the 1900s. I used to change buses at this corner in the early 1960s but when I visited in 1984 there were over 1000 people milling about.

Richard Chase was a collector of watercolor paintings by Colonel Francis Swain Ward, one of them being this painting of The Walajah Mosque at the Chepauk Palace in Madras around 1800.

4
MANSIONS AND MEMORIES

woman's home is her mansion, where she is the queen of her domain. We lived in many parts of India and in Sri Lanka, in many kinds of dwellings. I can only tell of my experiences and retell stories that were told to me by my parents and grandparents. I left India when I was 22, right after I completed college, so my memories are those of a young person, up to the end of college, from the beginning of the 1940s to the mid-1960s. President John Kennedy was elected president of the United States before I left India and he was assassinated two months after I arrived in America. It felt like time was slowing down. I have returned to India several times, but it's never the same. Additional facts and figures are easily accessible on the Internet. My personal recollections reside within me alone.

As I had never been to Katpadi, I always thought that my dad was born and raised in a village, but it is and was a thriving railway junction important to Anglo-Indians in the days of the Raj. Dad's father, my grandfather, Albert Chase worked for the railways.

In May of 1926, my dad went to work for the Imperial Bank of India in Madras on Mount Road. This is the Branch of the State Bank of India on (renamed) Anna Salai Road. He started as a clerk at the bank. He prided himself in his work and always taught us to be proud of whatever life brings us to do to earn a living. He was soon put in the Ledger section, which included writing daily updates in a big ledger. He wanted to be the best ledger writer, so he practiced copperplate lettering with his dipping-ink pen and became so good that his work was noticed, and he was promoted from that position. He notes in his diary that he worked on Ledgers 5 & 6. I would sure like to see them. Dad worked the ledgers in 1934 and then took a short leave to have a break. When he returned, he worked on Ledgers 1 & 2 and 3 & 4 until 1938, when he was promoted to Securities and then to Staff Assistant.

The State Bank of India Mt. Road branch in Madras.

By May of 1938, my dad was transferred to Bangalore as a Cash Passing Officer, where he met and married my mother. Their courtship was not without incident. One day, while they were sitting in the back of his car in a graveyard kissing, someone hurtled a large rock at them which went right through the rear window. They only survived because they looked out in opposite directions to see what the noise was. They would have been seriously injured if the rock had hit them. Public displays of affection are frowned on in India. Their relationship continued through over fifty years of married life. My dad noted in his family ledger in 1939 a simple "WWII" for the start of the horrific Second World War. On his wedding day he wrote in his diary the words "Lose my liberty." My mother put up some good arguments if things did not go the way she would like but mostly she allowed my dad to rule the family. We have some help remembering the dates of my dad's work and life moves, because he kept a minimal diary all his life, with exact dates of each transfer and life incident recorded for posterity. He kept a longer diary where he recorded his thoughts, quotations, and inspirational passages but this record of dates and work was sparce and to the point.

My father with his car in 1939.

I spent many years in Madras, coming back and coming back, as it has the strongest ties for me. I always say, "I'm from Madras," because I identify with this city the most. I was in Madras from the age of five to thirteen, with a short break when we went to Calcutta for a year. Later, after high school in Ooty, I returned and went to Queen Mary's College in Madras.

Every city and every town are special and different in so many ways. Every house we lived in was unique. I think the best way to give you a flavor of each place is to write my memories down. (If this piques your interest, I encourage you to check statistics and tourist venues online.) My dad said that Madras had a special smell because of all the spices; and that you could sense this aroma all the way from the outskirts of town in a junction known as Basin Bridge. Today, tomorrow, and yesterday blend in an alchemy that I can still taste, see, hear, and feel.

ELLORE (NOW ELURU) ON THE GODAVARI RIVER, IN ANDHRA STATE

My parents were still enjoying their honeymoon when they lived on a houseboat on the Godavari River in Andhra State near Ellore in 1940. It is a city that was built at the junction of the Krishna and Godavari River canal systems. My mother, who was only eighteen years old, told us later that everything imaginable would float by on this enormous river—once, even a dead body. My dad did inspections for the Imperial Bank at different facilities in the small towns along the riverbanks. It was cooler on the river than in their home in town, where the temperatures were often above 100°F, and they would pour buckets of water on the cement floor to cool it down. Their dog Rufus gave my mother company when my dad was out working. She became pregnant with me during these months on the Godavari River. I was conceived on the river, I come from the river and the Goddess Godavari. This city is mentioned in the ancient texts of the Mahabharata. My parents were in Ellore from February through June 1940 when they were transferred to Colombo, Ceylon.

Transfers. in Office

				Head Office
1st May 1926	—	Aug. 26	4. mths	Transfer Dept
Aug. 26	—	April. 27	9. ms	Pass Books
April 27	—	June 28	15. mths	Transfer
June 28	—	Jany 29	7 mths	Day Books
Jany. 29	—	July 1930	18 "	Bills
July 30	—	Dec. 1930	6. "	Stationery
Jany 31	—	May 1931	4. "	Leave
May 31	—	June 31	2. "	Shares
June 25th 31	—	Feby. 32	8 "	Counter Challan
Feby. 32	—	Jany 6th 1933	11 "	Savings Bk. Dfts
Jany 6 33	—	May 15 1933	4 "	Bills
May 15 33	—	Sep. 16	4. "	Ledgers 5 + 6
Sep 16 33	—	May 5 1934	8 "	D° 3.4 +CC
May 5 34	—	July 7 1934	2 "	Leave
July 7 34	—	Oct. 30, 1935	15 "	Ledger 1 + 2
Oct 11th 1935 Jany 5 1937	—	Feb. 10 1937	16 "	Assistant to Securities + also doing Miscellan work
Feb 10, 1937	—	1st March 1938	12/13 "	Securities Clerk
(Promoted as Staff Asst: 1.3.38)				
Mar. 2 1938	—	May 10 1938	2 "	HO. Supt: Drafts
May 10 1938	—	Feb 14 1940	21 "	Cash Passing Officer B'lor
Feb 17 — 1940	—	June 24 1940	4 "	Inspection duty Ellore

My dad's record of his transfers and work 1929-1939

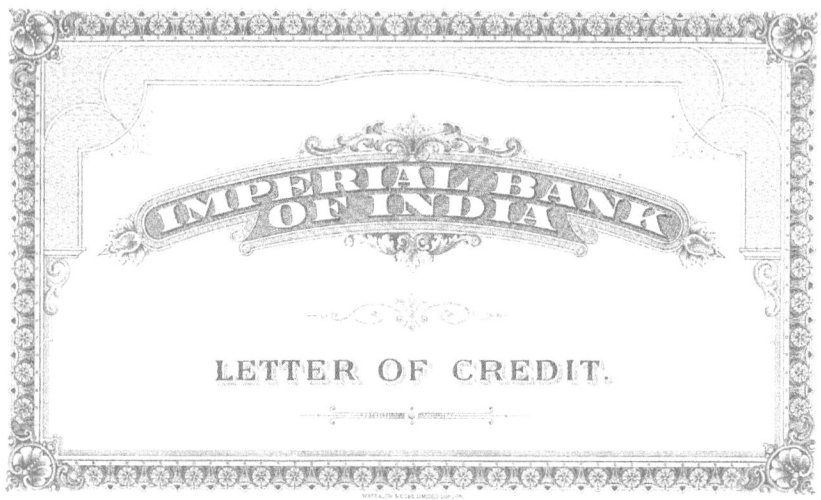

The Imperial Bank of India envelopes before it became the State Bank of India

TIRUPUR (TIRAPPUR) AND COIMBATORE (KOYAMBATOOR, KOVAI)

After a short stint in Colombo, Sri Lanka (formerly known as Ceylon), my parents moved to Tirupur in September of 1940. However, I was born in the General Hospital in Coimbatore. My mother, just nineteen years old, had to travel to Coimbatore for my birth. There was no hospital in Tirupur at that time. She stayed at a boarding house in Coimbatore, which was run by Anglo-Indians. She felt safe but she was worried because she had no idea how the baby was going to emerge. She awaited my birth alone. When I started to make an appearance, she was taken to the General Hospital for delivery. She was still very fearful, but also excited. She was fortunate to have an Anglo-Indian nurse, to whom I am indebted although her name is lost to us. This kind lady stayed after her shift to help my mother, who held onto her forearms so tightly they turned black and blue. My mother remembers my birth, at 101 she still has a crystal-clear mind.

On the Coimbatore station platform after I was born, coming home in 1940.

Coimbatore is a large, industrial city at the end of the drive down from the Nilgiris hills. It has cotton textiles, mills, and dyeing factories. There is a temple here, which was built about 600 years ago to the Goddess Koni Amma who is revered by the people in that area to this day. I returned to Coimbatore recently, driving late into the city that was all lit up. We stayed at a Residence hotel that was very modern in a grand Indian way. I felt that I had circled the earth to get there—in fact, I had. My circumnavigation was complete, and we flew out to Bangalore from Coimbatore.

My dad, who had to stay back in Tirupur to work, was informed of my birth and came down to Coimbatore by train to fetch my mother and me. Tirupur is an ancient city, as evidenced by artifacts retrieved from archeological sites. We returned to Tirupur from Coimbatore by train, but when we got to the station in Tirupur we had to take a horse-drawn cart (known as a jutkar vandi in Tamil and ghoda ghari in Hindi.) I arrived home in a cart, a carriage of sorts. My dad did not own a car in Tirupur, having sold his before their transfer to Colombo. From the time of my conception in Ellore to my birth in Coimbatore, ostensibly Tirupur, I had lived or been carried in utero in four cities and in two countries and travelled on a houseboat, a train, a ship, and a horse-drawn cart. It is not surprising that I countered all this early moving about by living in one city in America for over forty years.

My mother said that she only had three dresses at the time of my birth, which she rotated. My grandmother in Madras sourced a nanny, whom we called an ayah, a Portuguese word adopted by Anglo-Indians. This baby ayah ended up stealing and running away by train and was apprehended by the police on the way. That was the end of that! My great-grandmother Florence Lily Clapham came up from Bangalore to help my mother take care of me. I remember my great-grandmother later, when she was dying of cancer and lay in her bed in Bangalore in my grandmother's home. Here is where she died and was buried at Hosur Cemetery in 1946.

This was the simple house in Tirupur where I came after I was born in 1940.

The family also got a local woman to help, and she wore no blouse, as is the custom in that area of South India. She covered her breasts with her sari and carried on her work, sitting on the floor using grinding stones to smash the fresh spices and coconut for the curries that were made daily. The smell of those fresh green coriander leaves and mint being ground filled my olfactory senses, making an impression that seeped into my very being.

Tirupur is now known as the textile city of India because of its contribution to the cotton industry. However, the stories I was told over the years did not mention that. Nor did they tell of the ancient history of this town and its natural beauty on the fertile banks of the Noyyal River where agriculture thrived. It also has a mention in the Mahabharata. I was destined to be born in this area. My parents only lived in Tirupur from September before I was born until I was about 18 months old, and my dad was granted another leave then of about six weeks.

On a recent trip to India, we took the Heritage Blue Mountain train down the Nilgiri Ghats with views of deep gorges and big trees. The steam engine that pushed it up to Ooty acted as a brake to take us down to Metapalayam. Sivan, our taxi driver who had driven us down the hill roads, was waiting with his trusty Chevy to take us to the best dosai restaurant on our way to the Residency Hotel in Coimbatore. The hotel grounds covered about an acre, where it seemed that every bush, tree, and leaf was decorated with strings of lights for the new year. In Coimbatore, this city of my birth, even the towels at the hotel were perfumed with cardamom. A nice home coming that made me feel light, almost weightless.

TELLICHERRY (NOW THALASSERY)

Dad was transferred to Tellicherry in July of 1942, while the Second World War raged in Europe. The British had built a fort here in Tellicherry in 1708. This place had a breath-taking beach on the Malabar Coast where my parents enjoyed the sea breezes. My mother was modest, and the prevailing culture was such that it was difficult for a woman to get into a swimsuit and walk around; so, my dad made a tent from some bedspreads we called counterpanes. We had this tent for years. Dad later made a croquet set by hand and we would take it to large lawn spaces to play. There was a perfect one near the Cathedral in Madras where we would go as a family to play croquet. Back in Tellicherry, my mother would put on her swimsuit inside the counterpane-tent before enjoying the benefits of the fresh, healthy seawater. Afterwards she changed inside the tent again. My parents would then take down the tent, fold it up and take it home.

This may be the place where I got my love of the ocean and the beach. I think I inhaled the smell of that famous Tellicherry biriyani with its numerous spices that appeal to all the senses, too. It feels like you must be royalty to be honored with this amazing dish. The heavenly taste is beyond the usual everyday-dal-and-rice.

A photo of me in Tellicherry, standing next to our tent on the beach.

OOTACAMUND/UDAGAMANDALAM (POPULARLY KNOWN AS OOTY)

We lived in Ooty during the war in a small home, moving there in March of 1943. My sister was born from this home in the

Government Hospital on Hospital Road in 1944. When we returned together as adults, she refused to be photographed in front of the house. Of course, she didn't remember it as she was just a baby, but it was also very humble and over a century old. It was not a mansion by any means. I remembered it well, as I was almost five when we left. I have often drawn out the rooms and the outbuildings to stamp in my mind those memories. We did not have running water or city sewers. We had a room that was a bathroom with potties for each of us, mine being the littlest. The kitchen was down an outside corridor so the smoke from burning wood did not come into the house. I was often sent up with house staff to take my dad his tea at work. There was a grand entrance to the bank, but we would go straight up the hill from our house to the side of the bank to bring my dad some hot tea and a snack. He would come down the hill for lunch. I would dawdle over my lunch while I listened to my parents talk with tremors in their voices about the war or easily their supportive church events. I was always being punished for not eating my food with a spanking after which I was told to put on a happy face and eat faster next time. My heart felt full when, on Sundays, my dad would wrap his big blanket around us while he read stories to me from his large bible. The valley of dry bones in Ezekiel was one of my favorites. I vividly remember my mother being baptized as an adult in a small chapel at Montauban Guest House where they used to meet for services. This chapel was later moved to a church they built up on the hill and I often wonder how well people sleep in the renovated guest room now. So many baptisms, weddings and funerals occurred in that chapel.

Our beloved dog Rufus died in Ooty and was buried in the garden. In the market, he was involved in a fight with a rabid dog and acquired rabies that killed him. We were quarantined away from him and did not get rabies. Our sweet dog, Jill, had to be left behind in Ooty because of the cool climate she was used to.

One of my favorite memories was of the jalebi sweets lady who used to live on the earthen flat below our house. She would fire up her sigiri coal burner in the corner of the hillside and start cooking up those delicious jalebis. Their wonderful aroma would rise up the hillside and penetrate my senses. I still absolutely love jalebis. I would sit on my haunches up on the hill, all of four years old, and just watch her. She would call out and we would have a small exchange in Tamil until my mother found me missing. I would then be summoned inside —only to sneak out again the next time I smelled that delicious aroma. Later, the jalebi lady would soak these red round squiggles in sugar syrup and sell them in the market. There are many kinds of jalebis: jangiris made with red dal and brown raw sugar, imarti made with green cardamom and paneer, or cheese, jalebis. There may be other kinds, too, but the best are the regular crispy crunchy sweet jalebis made from yogurt-fermented flour, turmeric, saffron and a pinch of baking soda, fried in oil and then soaked in sugar syrup. These can be made from a mix or purchased ready-made. I am not sure if it is the actual food or the combination of the memories of certain foods and the foods themselves that make us love them so much. Jalebis conjure up both for me.

There was a tall cypress hedge that grew on the path to the Government Botanical Gardens in Ooty. As children we could play inside it. The same hedge seemed very, very tall when I was a young child, becoming smaller when I went back to Ooty as a teenager, and even smaller still, to normal size, when I became an adult. The garden itself was a grandly tiered and terraced wonder below Dodabetta Mountain. It had a small lookout towards the top which had a spectacular view of the whole garden. The Governor's Mansion was on one side and a Toda village was at the very top.

Breeks Memorial School in Ooty from the front (Times of India TOI photo).

I went back to Ooty to attend high school at Breeks Memorial School as a boarder in 1954, when my dad was again transferred to Sri Lanka. My mother attended this same school as a child. My parents felt this was the best decision because of the Singhalese language requirement in the schools in Sri Lanka. It soon became a rule in India that we were required to study the national language (Hindi) and the state language (Tamil), and I studied both. I can still mouth out words from the alphabets, but, without much active use of the languages, time has erased most of what I learned. When I am in Madras, I can pick up what people are saying but I am not fluent enough anymore to respond. I even studied Bengali when I was in Calcutta for a year. I studied French in college. I was annoyed on a visit to India, having brushed up on my Hindi, to find the words "MUNICIPAL BUILDING" spelled out in Devanagari script large and in lights. I was hoping to get the translation.

My friend Wendy and I at Breeks in 1956

It was difficult at first to be a boarder, but I did make life-long friends, many of whom I am still in touch with after all these years: Wendy, Fay, Eunice, Muriel, June, Toivo and others, and some of whom have passed on who I will always miss: Glenys, Chilly and Florence. These friends are close, tight inside my heart. We played netball in the clouds with the mist surrounding us, and went on picnics, hikes, and camping trips in this beautiful area of hilly terrain, pure rivers, and wide lakes. Ooty Lake was pristine then, and we would occasionally be allowed to take our bikes (mine was a Raleigh Sports) and circle the lake's many miles. We would also visit my friend Fay, whose parents lived on the premises of the palace belonging to the Nizam of Hyderabad. Fay was convinced that ghosts inhabited the palace and its many ancillary buildings, but I never saw any of them. The smell of eucalyptus, especially when it rained was a musty sweet scent that pervaded the air. The smoke pots used to distill the oil from the leaves which were heavily aromatic. Sometimes we would be taken on longer trips down the Ghats to Mysore or to the playing fields in Wellington for inter-school sports. One time, four of the boys from the school walked all the way up the hills until the soles of their shoes were worn out.

My friend Wendy and I with one of the boys, our friend Chilly, once got lost on a hike searching for a short cut across the hills. After meandering up hills and down dales, at dusk we finally came upon a chai teashop with a phone and called the school to give them our location. It was getting dark so we had begun to think of all the boy-scout ways we could survive the night outside. We felt our teen-age confidence, but the adults were very concerned for us and happy to be reunited.

We went camping by waterfalls and rivers. Trout had been seeded in the streams. Reading out loud was a nice recreational activity before the Internet and other multi-media distractions. I listened to The Lion, the Witch, and the Wardrobe, (the first book in the Chronicles of Narnia by C.S. Lewis) which had recently been released and pondered its many possible allegories. We warmed up with a fire after almost being blown off a cliff by strong winds while hiking earlier. At night, we heard the trumpeting of elephants. The purple Strobilanthes flowers covered the hills with their beauty. It was a magical time.

Mine wasn't the first generation in my family to live in the Nilgiris. My mother was born in Wellington, as were some of her siblings: Many of them were christened at St. Georges Garrison Church in Wellington including Len, Lionel, Eddie, Gwen and Audrey. Her family lived in Ooty, too, when my grandmother had a boarding house for a while, and they attended St. Thomas' Church where my uncle, Charlie is buried. My grandfather, Harry, retired from the Army and worked in the Cordite Factory in Aruvankadu which is still part of the Indian Defense services. My grandfather had a Tin Lizzie that he later sold at auction for one rupee. However, the new owner could not drive well and he turned it over in their front yard before he could take it away.

The Imperial Bank of India now the State Bank on First Line Beach, Madras

We went from Ooty to Madras in 1945 and I went to kindergarten in Madras the following year. Our school had been taken over by the army, so we attended at a nearby convent.

TRICHINOPOLY (NOW TIRUCHIRAPPALLI)

The city of Trichinopoly is on the banks of the Cauvery River. I did not know that it is famous for Trichies, a rich cigar known as Black Tiger Cigars that was once smoked by Winston Churchill. My experience in this town was as a stopping place between boarding school and home, the school being in Ooty and home in Colombo, Ceylon (Sri Lanka). We took the Blue Mountain Nilgiris Express from Ooty, changed trains at Mettupalayam and went on to Trichinopoly. There we sat in the waiting room all day until we could get on a train to the island nation to the south. While we sat in the waiting rooms, a nice Anglo-Indian lady who was the attendant taught me to make the most exquisite paper flowers, which was her avocation. The train then went over land and water to the capital city of Colombo. Once, while traveling during the rainy season, the train jogged slowly, inch by inch, on flooded tracks that were barely visible in those murky, yard-deep waters, but we got home safely. After that fairly dangerous journey we flew home on a Viscount or a DC3. We didn't venture out into the city, and I wished we had met people or seen the sites. My aunt Thelma's family came from Trichy, the Rickets.

COLOMBO IN CEYLON (NOW SRI LANKA)

In mid-1940, when my mother was pregnant with me, my parents lived in a boarding house in Colombo. My father worked for the bank as he did for his whole career. They did not enjoy Ceylon and transferred back after a few months. My dad had to request a return to India. That's when he was sent to Tirupur, where I would have been born if they had a hospital back then.

My parents, Isabel, and Stephen in the early 1950s

Sri Lanka, or Ceylon, had an interesting history. It was under Portuguese rule from 1505-1658, and under Dutch rule from 1658-1796. Then the British took over, until 1948 when Sri Lanka gained independence. There are also the Tamils, who came down from India and live mostly in the north, and their own indigenous people, the Singhalese. As a result, there are Hindus, Buddhists, and Christians, including Roman Catholics, Protestants and Dutch Reformed. The people of mixed heritage seem to lean mostly to their Dutch roots, although the Portuguese culture is also a strong influence.

Period	Months	Department
27th June 1940 to 7th Sep. 1940	2. 10 days	4th Passing Officer. Colombo.
9th Sep 1940 to Dec 1940	3. Mo	Ag. Ass. Acct. Tirupur
Dec 1940 to 26th May 1942	15 Mo	Holding Gold – Dec. 1940 / Holding Cash – Dec – 1941
26 May 1942 to 13th July 1942	1½ Mo	Leave
13th July 1942 to 12th Mar 1943	8 M	Agent – Tellicherry.
13 Mar 1943 to 13 Sep 1945	2½ Ys	Ag/Acctt – Ootacamund
14th Sep 1945 to 14th Nov 1945	2 Mo	Leave
14th Nov 1945 to 14th Jany 1948	24 Mo	Passing Officer, Madras
15th Jany 1948 to 29th Jany 1948	2 wks	Deputy Acctt
29th Jany 1948 to 16th Nov 1948	9½ Mo	Foreign Exchange Deptt
17th Nov 1948 to 16th Feby 1949	3 Mo	Leave.
17 Feby 1949 to 3rd June 1950	16 Mo	P.E.D. Madras.
4 June 1950 to 1st Mar 1951	9 ms	– Calcutta.
5th Mar 1951 to 21st Apl 1953	2 yp 16 days	– Madras
22nd Apl 1953 to 11th Aug 1953	4 ms	Leave – U.K.
12th Aug 1953 to 26th Apl 1954	8 ms	P.E.D. Madras.
28th Apl 1954 to 3rd July 1954	2½ ms	Acctt. Colombo.
5 July 1954 to 21st Mar 1957	2 yp 9 ms	Sub Agent Colombo
22nd Mar 1957 to 2nd Apl 1957	11 days	Leave.
3rd Apl 1957 to 2nd Aug 1958	16 ms	Agent, Alleppey.

Dad's list of transfers and job titles from 1940-1958

In April of 1954 my dad was transferred to Colombo again. This time he stayed for three years. It was a much more enjoyable move. My dad was first the Accountant and then the Sub-Agent (Vice Branch Manager). We had a very large apartment overlooking the harbor and the ocean, with a deep patio where my dad grew bougainvillea, hibiscus, and fuchsias in purple and pink. We saw the ocean liner, the Queen Mary, docked for a while long before it was retired and docked at Long Beach in California.

My mother was pregnant again, fifteen years after her first foray in Ceylon. My two sisters had been born in the interim, Margo in Ooty and Jenny in Madras. This time she had a boy, my brother, and much-anticipated son, Eric. I was away in boarding school in Ooty when he was born where we received a joyous telegram announcing his birth. It came while I was at school and my sister opened it, told the whole group of boarding girls and they waited in hiding for me. When I returned, they all yelled: "It's a boy! It's a boy!" That's actually how I found out I had a brother, not from the telegram from my parents.

My dad was extremely strict with us. I remember getting a beating for accidentally leaving the gas spigot open after my bath. I was about fifteen years old then, and it was the last time I was chastised in this way. I asked my dad how old I was when he started spanking me, or correcting me, with a wooden ruler. He answered that I was only 15 months old. As I was still nursing my children when they were that age, I couldn't imagine beating a baby or what I could possibly have done wrong at so young an age. But my father was set in his Victorian beliefs, always with

The State Bank of India in Colombo, Sri Lanka.

the aid and support of my mother. We were raised in a strict and God-fearing family; but we also feared our parents, which is how we were kept on the narrow and straight path.

We belonged to a local informal church, a Brethren Assembly, where my dad often preached, and my mother made many friends and learned to cook some Sri Lankan dishes. The Poulier sisters influenced my mother, and we enjoyed their cooking. A few of their recipes and ideas were memorialized later in the many cookbooks by their niece, the much-honored Charmaine Solomon. The equivalent of the Anglo-Indian community was the Dutch Burgher people who were of mixed Portuguese, Dutch, British and Sri Lankan heritage. We enjoyed the Dutch Burgher specialties: honey-infused Love Cake and the dense Dutch Breudher yeast bread that was often made on New Year's Eve. The church groups had many get-togethers and parties, and we were involved with the YMCA that had programs for young people. My mother designed and sewed our dresses. I was lucky because I got two dresses for the holiday season, as my birthday was at the end of November and Christmas came soon after. I still have those sugar-floss-like nylon dresses, packed away in a box: a yellow one with a yellow satin slip and a pink one that also has a matching slip. It has been a long time since they were in style (and since I could fit into them) but here they are.

Our bank-owned living quarters was up on the fourth floor at the top of the bank building. As kids we had fun operating the old elevator and playing hide and seek along the corridors in front of the other apartments. The Pettah Markets, spilling over the sidewalks, were an exciting place to haggle over brightly dyed cloth or kitchen wares. The Galle Face green is a large maidan (open field) on the oceanfront. I loved to watch the sunsets there, mottled with blacks and reds, oranges, and pinks. I learned that these unusual sunsets had been created by an eruption of the volcano Krakatau in Indonesia, which spewed volcanic dust into the sky. My mother is unsentimental, and she decried my enjoyment of these sunsets. I love to walk on the beach or ocean paths. Luckily, so did my dad, and I was occasionally able to indulge this interest with him while my mother shopped at stores nearby.

My dad had a gun in his desk, not that he knew how to use it. Sri Lanka was a violent country then and known to have more murders per capita than the city of Chicago. Once, he was on an inspection in a distant location and went there with a driver. Upon completing the job, he directed his driver to return home by a certain route. As the story was told, the driver communicated with him using a matchbox that a couple of thugs were going to follow their car and try to rob them, so they quietly went another direction and avoided this catastrophe.

Dad went up to the temple town of Kandy in 1956, during the Buddha Jayanti, which commemorated the 2500th anniversary of the Buddha's birth and life. He took many photographs of these spectacular Buddhist cultural events. However, when my brother got ill at home and due to my dad's strong Christian beliefs, he felt compelled to destroy the photos, so these no longer exist.

We lived by the harbor in Colombo, and I sang *Harbor Lights*, a 1950 hit song, constantly that year. "I saw the harbor lights, they only told me we were parting..." People left for England, often by sea. I loved listening to my then-boyfriend play the piano, but he left with his mother for England and my love was gone forever. All I had was his signature in my autograph book. His and Lord Mountbatten's signatures reside there. I had acquired Lord Mountbatten's signature by bribing staff at the Governor's mansion in Ooty, along with many other students.

Signatures of the Earl of Mountbatten and Edwina from my autograph book

Our home in Colombo was in the financial district. From here we could look down onto department stores that were owned by British companies. Across to the harbor we could see large ships. There was a saloon down below in our building towards the back, and I often listened to the tinkling of live jazz music wafting up to my window. Sometimes we would hear the loud vulgar shouts of drunken English sailors, too. Even then, there were many murders and urban disruptions going on in the city down below us.

We had a Burmese teakwood trunk with brass trimmings on a stand. It was meant for liquors, but since my family did not drink or offer alcohol to guests, my mother used it for her needlework. She was an accomplished seamstress and made all our clothes, except for our school uniforms that were made by a tailor. A room next to the kitchen was filled with fragile china and glassware belonging to the bank. My father had inventoried all these treasures and kept them locked up to prevent damage. We used to have cases of soft drinks delivered to our house and sometimes went into town to buy Lyons' ice cream from England.

Road trip in Sri Lanka in 1956 with my sisters and dad.

My family made trips into other areas of Ceylon, areas that were peaceful at that time. Dad brought along a friend when he took us three girls to see some historic sites. Many of these sites are now on the World Heritage register. We visited the ancient capital of Anuradhapura, and Polonnaruwa with its many relics and stone statues. We saw some colossal statues of Buddha carved into the stone. My dad travelled without hotel reservations and would stop at a favorable hotel at dusk. We tried several in Polonnaruwa but could not find rooms. Finally, Dad convinced a hotel staff to put down mattresses in their living area on the stipulation that we be gone before breakfast. We drove through Kandy where we bought coconut water straight from the green coconuts and sugar cane juice squeezed from the cane on the spot. These were the safest, cleanest, and most refreshing drinks to be had.

Then, on to the Peradeniya botanical gardens, the scene of many movies including *The Bridge Over the River Kwai*, *Indiana Jones and the Temple of Doom* and *Elephant Walk*, this last was filmed in 1953 and starred Elizabeth Taylor. We stopped at the walled city of Galle (a city that was hit hard much later by the tsunami), and we drove to the beaches of Trincomalee, which were scattered with purple and white coral shells. At Sigiriya we climbed 200 feet up the ancient rock to see the palace ruins on top. It was single file up steps cut into the stone dome. From the top we could see all over the valley. It was raining in the distance, although it was sunny on the rock. We watched as the rain came towards us and drenched us because we would not risk descending the wet steps. Sri Lanka is a rich green island, beautiful in all its parts.

HYDERABAD (THE NEWLY FORMED TELANGANA STATE FORMERLY HYDERABAD STATE)

My family lived in the city of Hyderabad for almost a year from 1959 to 1960. My father was the Bank Manager there. The bank was on the ground floor of the building and the bank manager's quarters were in the expansive upstairs apartment. There was a beautiful, gleaming, circular marble staircase that joined the two floors. My brother, Eric, was around four years old and already given to terrorizing us in his own way. One time, he threw a toy down the well of the stairs. That was probably fun, but my sister, Margo, felt he had to go down (by himself) to pick up the toy, and, on her way, she called out terror on him to do so. Hearing the yelling and crying and whatnot, I came to see what was happening. Then I snuck back into the house and asked one of the staff to go around by the back stairs to help, which he did. Upstairs, the formal living room was a huge hall. To make the large room feel a bit more closed in and cozy, my mother ordered deep pink drapes to be tailored for each and every door—there must have been six or eight. Beyond this room was a formal dining room where we had our meals. Beyond that, there was an English billiards room with a large billiards table and all the accoutrements (like balls and cue sticks) plus a two-row gallery for onlookers. It was quite elegant, but my parents did not play and locked up the room, so that was that. I was already away at college in Madras, but I spent my summers in Hyderabad and they were hot. The walls of the building were made of stone.

My dad, at his office downstairs, had a khus-khus screen over the door like a curtain, which was constantly wetted down by the staff peons. The heady scent of the khus-khus grass roots kept the room fresh and cool. My mother ordered all the beds to be placed on the wide veranda so that we could enjoy the cool night air. My actual bedroom was by the marble stairway and a midnight knock woke me one night. It was a telegram delivery informing us of a cousin's death. My dad explained that this part of the family had moved north to the ancient city of Meerut and to the railway junction Bhusawal, through which most major train routes in India pass. Some members of my mother's family on the Lilywhite side still live in this town.

There was a long row of bamboo on the grounds of the Hyderabad bank. It must have been over one-hundred feet long and at least thirty feet high. The bamboo trunks were thick, about eight inches around. We were told that it would flower only once in a hundred years and then die; but no one could tell us if they'd ever seen it flower.

We often drove into Hyderabad's twin city, Secunderabad. It had a large railway station built of stone, too, like the bank where we stayed. We went to see the Salar Jung Museum in Hyderabad many times with guests. It was—and still is—very impressive with many artifacts from Europe and Asia collected by Nawab Mir Yousuf Ali Khan, also known as Salar Jung.

CALCUTTA (KOLKATA)

We moved to Calcutta from Madras by train, and we also sent our black Ford V8 that weighed exactly one ton—with its shiny wheel hubs and sideboards—ahead (by train). The track went straight up 1000 miles from Madras to Calcutta. The train line ran parallel to the Grand Trunk Road, up the country from south to north and back. The Grand Trunk Road may have sprung from the old Silk Road, which had its beginnings in antiquity. Merchants would travel all the way from China to Turkey and Europe carrying big packs of goods on their backs or on their heads. India was a wide and long detour.

We lived in Calcutta from 1950 to 1951, where I attended Pratt Memorial School. The children at this school played lots of games. In one, I stood in a circle with classmates, all concentrating on a person who was in the middle until that person fell in a certain direction. Then it was on to the next girl in the circle. We lay on the grass and stared at the clouds, figuring out what the different formations resembled. My parents had the high life and were invited to formal and informal parties. My mother had a dress made for formal occasions from an expensive material called sharkskin which was smooth and soft. It was a beautiful dress of a light ivory color that suited her well. She sometimes wore it with a corsage of lilies. We used to attend "church" in the apartment of a friend of my parents in a ritzy neighborhood. Little bands of bagpipers often serenaded us from the street below. My parents' friends were Armenians who belonged to a large Armenian population in Calcutta. There was a big Chinatown, too, which was all lit up at night and where we sometimes went for dinner. One time my whole family was invited to a dinner party at an

Englishman's home. Drinks were flowing. This was 1951 and there were many British bankers still in India. A bearer (staff) would come around and pour drinks while the guest looked away and then looked back at the last moment to tell the man "Bas, bas" meaning enough in Hindustani. At that dinner, I was given a beautiful, leather-bound copy of Little Women by Louisa May Alcott which I still have.

Quetta, north of Calcutta, is known for its earthquakes. The largest was in 1935 when over 30,000 people died. When we lived in Calcutta there was an earthquake as far away as Quetta and we felt it in Calcutta. We all piled out of our apartment building (where we were living on the top floor) and stood on the maidan, watching the ceiling fans swing back and forth. When it was over, we returned upstairs only to find the cook and staff sitting on the floor in the kitchen playing cards, having not felt a thing. I liked visiting that coal-burning kitchen, sitting on the spiral iron stairs out back, and looking out on the city. I have nightmares now thinking of how unsafe it must have been, but I enjoyed the cool air, confident in my dexterity then.

Calcutta was a big, crowded city. My dad had been warned not to stop if he ever had an accident, but to move his car as fast as possible away from the scene. One day an elderly woman walked deliberately into our car from the front and started yelling that she was hurt and that it was Dad's fault. A crowd gathered. Fortunately, because of my father's presence of mind and being forewarned, he was able to maneuver the car out of the crowd and we made it home.

Calcutta is well known for its congested streets with traffic of every kind. There were ten lanes of cars in a street designed for four. Inevitably, there were accidents. One time, my mother kept calling out "Don't look! Don't look!" to us children, who were supposed to close our eyes. I peeked, of course, but I wish I had not. My mother was crying in the front seat, and the driver was trying to make headway out of the sad mess. A person had been killed, but the body was unrecognizable, just creamed into small bits of flesh and bone, a terrible, unforgettable scene.

We could see the famous Durga festival from the window of our flat. Huge crowds of people, chanting and singing mantras, moved slowly toward the river, following the saffron-robed priests and the fancily, ritually dressed idol. It was a spectacular scene to watch.

My father, as I have mentioned, had a Victorian approach to raising children. He often quoted the proverbial phrase "spare the rod and spoil the child," which he assumed was permission from God to beat his children. It was hard for me to find love in his corporal punishment over the years of my childhood. It was in Calcutta that he administered the most severe punishment of my young life. When I was eleven, there was a companiable group of children living with their parents on the grounds of the college where we had rented an apartment. There were vast grassy fields and structures, like abandoned building foundations, in which we could hide and play. I teamed up with the oldest boy, Premen, and we would lead the other children in playing some organized games, like hide and seek. We had so much fun and ran and ran all over that campus, which was walled in and safe for us.

One evening my dad asked me to go down two floors to the dark basement where his car was parked, open the car and find a pair of his gloves. I was so scared. When I got there, I could not find a light switch, so I fumbled around in the foreboding darkness. Not finding the gloves immediately, I ran upstairs with my heart in my throat to tell him, hoping he would help me. My father was furious. He was certain that my confusion was because I was playing too much with the boy next door. I got a severe beating and was further told I could never speak to my friend again. His mother taught me the piano, so this was doubly difficult. We would sometimes whisper on the stairs, but all the fun had ended. We were soon transferred back to Madras, but I always missed that friendship and could never figure out how it was connected to my fright in the basement garage and my dad's incomprehensible fury. Perhaps he had started to feel the weight of protecting my virginity, even at that young age. A weight that could only be understood by another Victorian-thinking Indian.

ALLEPPEY (ALAPPUZHA) AND COCHIN (KOCHI) IN KERALA

We travelled around the country via transfers and vacations. We lived in Alleppey in 1957, in a mansion with deep verandas. The whole house shuddered during the tropical storms of Kerala, which made me want to flee or hide but there was nowhere safer to go. My dad was walking towards the kitchen one day (he rarely went there) and in a flash a lightning bolt skipped in front of him. It did not hit or kill him but an inch closer and it could have. A huge clap of thunder followed and rain, heavy monsoon rain. Thunderstorms in that area of Kerala are formidable. This house was old, maybe a hundred years old. The rooms were large with anterooms and a wide, veranda that stretched all along the front of the house. We spent most of our days on this veranda, often listening to the news on Voice of America. There was a large porch in front with a balcony above.

Bank house in Allepey ,1958. It is now a bank, and the verandas are boarded up.

I passed the time after high school reading most of Shakespeare's plays and a rare novel I could purchase with my pocket money from a little bookstore that sold English language paperback books. We listened to the BBC news on the radio. I slept in a room that should have been a dressing room, but I liked its cozy, sunny location. My parents had the room on the other side, and they used their dressing room as a nursery, where my little brother slept. The second bedroom, which could have been mine, was very dark, being shaded by the large veranda. This dressing room with an attached bathroom had a window facing the front of the house over the car portico and another that opened onto a stair landing. I had a lovely circular mosquito net over my bed that I cherished sleeping under. The billowing white mosquito nets were custom made for each bed. The second bedroom, being vacant, attracted all kinds of activity. I had to go through that bedroom to access my bedroom. I would jump out the window onto the stairs to exit sometimes—but not to enter. I heard later that the baby ayah (maid) had been fired because she was having an affair with the bearer in that spare bedroom when they were supposed to be working. Not that I knew any of that at the time.

I lived in Alleppey after I completed my Senior Cambridge High School Certificate from Breeks Memorial School in Ooty, so I had no friends in this town. My friends had scattered to the various continents which their parents came from originally. In fact, my mother had very few friends here either, because the church my parents attended was a Malayalam Assembly that only translated services to English when my father was present. In their tradition, only men could participate in the services, so the women were relegated to the sidelines. The congregation was seated in separate sections for men and women. My brother was very small, so one of my parents stayed home with him each week. Since this created a problem for the translator, we decided to always have my dad attend and my mother and I stayed home alternately to babysit my brother.

The bank staff with our family in Allepey 1958 (Me with my brother in front.)

There was a large roof top deck over the portico that cars drove under when arriving at our house. When my brother was two years old, I took many photographs of him on this terrace, posing with this and that—encyclopedias, telephones, and such. He was a very active little boy, so it was not easy. My dad took a video of him eating a banana which he was simultaneously sharing with our goat. The whole large property was fenced in. In one spot the fence jutted out in a triangular shape, where a big tree had been preserved and grew even larger. There was an enormous cashew nut tree in the front side-yard. Cashews grow outside their apple-like fruit. Because of their bitter oil, they cannot be picked and peeled by anyone except those who know how to do it properly after the fruit is dried in the sun. My mother used to get these fresh raw cashew nuts and sauté them in a pan until they were a glossy light brown. She served them after dinner with a little salt, maybe a dash of chili pepper. They were very good with a cup of tea to finish off the meal.

We had some pigs at this house. My mother loved them, I thought. She fed them herself every day but when we had to leave, she had them slaughtered and cooked into a vindaloo which I refused to taste. Our cook used to make the best buttermilk for me. It was salty, not sweet. He would make the buttermilk fresh and finish it off with sautéed black mustard seeds and curry leaf to make a satisfying drink. This was part of my mother's plan to fatten me up so that I would get married. She was convinced that I was too thin. Her concern transferred to me—not that I wanted to get married then, but just to look the part. She also made a ginger drink with chilies called O.T., usually made for Christmas as a non-alcoholic alternative. I would drink this a half an hour before dinner to give me a better appetite. I was really not interested in eating in those days.

When I was in America and was contemplating a trip back home to India, I went to see a doctor to help me gain weight so that I would be more acceptable body-wise at my sister's wedding. He told me to "just carry around a sack of potatoes" for all the good gaining weight would do for my health. The weight would come as I got older, but I didn't know that then. My mother also took me to several doctors to find out why my breasts were not growing larger, but that's another story.

Towards the back of the land around the house, my dad grew vegetables that we ate fresh-picked with meals. When my mother went on a trip once for about a month, Dad gave our cook one order: fried eggs for breakfast, curry and rice for lunch, and vegetable cutlets for dinner. Repeat daily.

On the drive from Madras to Alleppey, my mother was taking her turn at the wheel. Dad snoozed beside her, and my brother, a toddler, sat in the back surrounded by padded hold-alls that were rolled up and tied with straps (like sleeping bags). Mom veered off the road and Dad woke up and over-corrected the car, which rolled over three times down an embankment. They all survived. A whole village surrounded them as they crawled out of the broken windshield with only scratches. My brother was fine, wrapped as he was in cotton puffery. The villagers did not touch a thing. Someone found my dad's wallet in the wreckage and handed it to him. They were taken to the closest bank manager's quarters to wait until they found alternate transportation to their destination, where dad was to start work as the manager of the Alleppey bank. He was probably only the first or second Indian branch manager after Independence, as there was still a British contingency living in Allepey—planters, managers, and their wives.

When I was sixteen, I came to Alleppey over the September

holidays to study for my Senior Cambridge Certificate final exams. September holidays were a hangover from Michaelmas, an extension of the Feast of St. Michael holiday that the British observed. I took a train from Ooty to Coimbatore with some friends from school who were also going that way. My friends stopped in Coimbatore, and I took a plane from there to Cochin, which was as far as it went. My parents could not pick me up at the airport because their car was still being repaired. A friend of my parents was to arrive on the same plane as me and would have their car and driver at the airport. I was supposed to be given a ride with this friend. However, they ended up not taking that plane and the driver never found me (or maybe he didn't look very hard, I don't know.) In those days, I would have stood out as a single young woman travelling alone. I always got airsick on planes, as was the case on this day, so I was not thinking very clearly, either. I took a cab to the Malabar Hotel, famous even then. (Later after the car was fixed, we would sometimes go to this hotel to use their pool and swim and play in the water for a few hours.) I had lunch at the hotel but could only eat soup and toast because I was still feeling ill. Then, I asked the hotel concierge (the front desk manager) to call my dad on a long-distance call to the bank to let them know I was safe. After I got directions to Alleppey, I went to the dock and boarded a boat—along with the village women and their baskets and chickens—and crossed the river. Don't ask me which river or canal it was now! It was probably the wide Periyar River. I then got a bus. It started to rain like it can only rain in Kerala and went on and on and on. A man on the bus tried to befriend me and told me I should get off, but I was afraid he would kidnap me for sure. I rode the bus to the end of the line, then hired a rickshaw and set out to find the Bank House in Alleppey. Finally, a man who said he was a clerk at the bank said he knew where the house was. He rode alongside the rickshaw on his bicycle until we found the house. My mother came running out of the house. She and my dad acted like I had come down from heaven, they were so glad to see me. I thought I did just fine and never thought that I was lost at all.

It was in Alleppey that my dad taught me to drive. We went out in his Morris Minor (or maybe it was the Austin Healey). I remember it as a Morris not an Austin, but my siblings remember differently—although they were very young at the time and mostly repeat stories the way they remember them being told. We drove over the bunds between the rice paddies in the fields on the outskirts of town. My dad impressed on me three important rules of driving in India: One, never swerve for a chicken because you may hit a child. Two, always straddle cow dung to keep from messing up your car and wheels. And three, don't shine your lights on a bullock cart because the ox could shy and the yoke might swing out and hit your windshield, possibly killing you. When I came to America, I had to learn to drive on the other side of the road, but I never forgot these three rules for driving in India, even when they became pretty useless to me (and even to people in India in the cities).

From Alleppey, my dad was transferred to Cochin where we lived during 1958 and 1959. This was near the Navy Base in Ernakulam where we made many friends. I turned 18 that year and enjoyed going to the dinners with my parents at the Navy Officer's Club where I met many young navy officers. There was one I particularly hit it off with, but my parents would never allow us to be alone together. They took their chaperoning duties too seriously.

The bank house in Cochin was a mansion more modern than the one in Alleppey. It was beautifully designed with gleaming teakwood everywhere. Windows faced the ocean across one side of the bedrooms, with teak shutters to block the noonday sun. There were large almirahs (armoires), made of Burmese teak and rosewood. There was a four-poster bed in my bedroom with mosquito netting that was put down in the evening, and plenty of room for my little dog to run around the bed. My mother had the teak dining table and chairs put out on the veranda, facing the ocean, for breakfast—Chotta, as we called it. Chotta haazri was a small, early morning meal. Ships would go by this house with a band playing if perhaps an admiral was on board, and at night the ship would be all lit up like a floating hotel.

Nearby, so close you could look down into it from the side bedroom windows, was a very old Dutch graveyard with weeds and ivy growing over the graves with Dutch names on them from the 1700s. It might be the oldest cemetery of European graves in India. An old Dutch church was down the street. It is named for St. Francis and Vasco de Gama was buried there in 1524. He was later exhumed and reburied in Portugal. There were Dutch and English graves inside St. Francis Church, flush with the flooring. The stone memorials were poignant, taking visitors back through the centuries. At Willingdon Island, where Fort Cochin was built, they have artifacts from the Portuguese and Dutch. I was told that if you could chop off a piece of a table there and soak it in water it would turn into pure gin from all the Dutch gin jenever that it had soaked up. (Of course, no one would really dare to try this!)

Here in Alleppey, the soaring oft-pictured Chinese fishing nets were not far from where we lived. They are a timeless beauty to see, especially at sunset. At a little shop near a wealthy Jewish section where our doctor lived, I bought a beautiful silver bracelet with ivory elephants as a reminder of the first article I ever had published. I still have it. This area is not to be confused with Jew Town, which was established hundreds of years before. I visited our Dr. Kotta's house once or twice. It was very large, laid out in a square with an open courtyard in the middle and was three stories high. A grand place.

BANGALORE (BENGALURU)

My mother, remembering a time before she was married, wrote to my cousin Greg: "I am positive that we moved to Bangalore in early 1938 or late 1937. We went to a house on Rest House Road near MG Road (previously South Parade) and then shifted to 29 Norris Road and later to 3 Alexandria St in Richmond Town. That's where I met my husband and married in 1939." You can find these locations on Google Maps and Google Earth, although most of those old houses are gone. Some of those old street names are still used: Myrtle Lane, Clapham Street, Serpentine Street, Wellington Street and Walker Lane. My maternal grandparents and several of my aunts also lived in Bangalore as did my great-grandmother and my great great-grandparents. Bangalore is our home.

Dr. Marrett's Gospel Hall in Richmond Town, Bangalore.

We stayed with Dr. Marrett's son Stanley no's and his family on a holiday in 1948. I am still friends with Dr. Marrett's grandchildren, Dorothy, and Faith. There was a large compound and I remember Haley's Comet overhead, and a lady who was affected by the full moon and other celestial phenomena, walking up and down the garden, calling out and crying. Poor lady. Dr. Marrett had a dispensary across from the church. These are still there, but with new owners and new buildings. We have one photo from that time which I only recently discovered; it seems to have everyone we knew in it. I celebrated my eighth birthday during that holiday and got a lovely red purse, which shows up in many photos. (It is the same purse that enticed a pet monkey to bite me later.)

My dad was transferred to Bangalore while I was attending college in Madras. He was the manager of the Bangalore Branch of the State Bank of India from 1960 to 1962.

We lived in the large accommodations above the bank, on a twelve-acre property with a cottage on one side where the Chief Accountant lived. Dad had promised my mother that by the time he was ready to retire, they would live in that cottage. However, by that time the British (who kept all the prestigious positions for themselves) had left India and my dad was promoted to manager, we lived in the big mansion.

My parents' wedding on June 14, 1939, at the Gospel Hall in Richmond Town.

This was a very special home. Named Hopeville, it is about 160 years old now. It was built for Sir Mark Cubbon when he was the Resident of Mysore State (Commissioner of Mysore territories) which included Bangalore. Sir Mark Cubbon served in the East India Company during the first half of the nineteenth century. There is still, I believe, a statue of him on a horse in front of the high courts in Bangalore. Cubbon Park, in Bangalore, was also named after him. Saunders Road in Bangalore was named for Charles Burslam Saunders, who lived at Hopeville when he was the Resident after Sir Mark Cubbon resigned. Carrie Butler wrote to me to tell me that her grandparents and family lived in this house when her grandfather, Norman Patrick Mithen, was the deputy bank manager around 1920. It is said that this beautiful home was purchased by the Madras Bank for only 30,000 Rupees from Charles James Green, a retired Major General of the Madras Army, in 1864.

My daughters, Natala and Sheila, taken showing the tennis courts in the 1980s at Hopeville

When walking up the staircase, a window with the Union Jack in stained glass is illuminated at the top. Twelve-foot-tall carved Burma teak doors open into a large hall which comprises the living and dining areas as well as a reception area with views of the trees beyond. Bats sometimes flew in at night. Monkeys lived in the trees and occasionally jumped on to the veranda looking for a banana or mango to eat. The trees themselves were large and spreading. The house is storied to have a secret passage to Cubbon Park.

Taken in 1962 when my dad was the manager of the Bangalore branch of the State Bank of India with Hopeville in the background.

Hopeville has five large bedrooms, five baths, two large living rooms and a huge dining room. It had big high doors and deep verandas and terraces. There are four towering Tuscan-style column pillars at the entrance with an enormous balcony above forming a carriage driveway.

Hopeville inside showing the dining area.

The building itself, which is built in the Residency style, was an architectural inspiration for other buildings in Bangalore such as the Raj Bhavan and the Bangalore Club. It was filled with furnishings, paintings and artifacts dating back to the days of Mark Cubbon. When I was there, I would walk just to the gate and back with my little dog. Now there are many cottages facing Residency Road, and a new bank on the corner of St. Mark's Road. I often walked to that side, too, crossing over to the British Library to borrow books. It was a beautiful bungalow and grounds.

Myself on the balcony of Hopeville with my friend Faith Marrett circa 1961.

I developed a love of bank vaults, growing up in the atmosphere of banks. In those days, the rupees were counted by hand and clerks would sit out at tables counting all the packets of crisp new-smelling money. They became very efficient at this, almost as fast as the modern-day machines. I loved to visit the vault with my dad. Sometimes there were large deposits of chunky gold jewelry and intricately carved and fashioned gold ornaments. There were always guards and mirrors to monitor visitors to the low-ceilinged dark-walled bank vault where there would be a television now.

This photo of me was taken in front of Hopeville in the 1980s.

Dad was transferred back to Madras before I left India. He retired as the Chief Accountant of the Head Office Madras State of the State Bank of India, a prestigious position. The family got to live in Bangalore again after he retired in 1966. My parents and my brother emigrated from India in May of 1967, and they started a new life in Australia.

Going further back, my great-great-grandfather Mathew Clapham was the Inspector of Schools in Bangalore around 1880. He is mentioned in *The Report on Public Instruction in Mysore*, for the year 1877-78 before he became inspector. He was transferred to Mysore as an acting headmaster at the Normal School where he is noted as having "introduced order and regularity into everything and…under his management the school will become of the best district schools in Mysore." I'm sure his hard work and dedication was recognized when he was made inspector for the whole state.

My mother, Isabel, on the stairs of Hopeville in Bangalore on a visit in the 1980s.

Mathew Clapham's father (my great-great-great-grandfather) was the Chief of Police (so I've been told), now known as the Police Commissioner of Bangalore City. One story goes that my great-great-great-grandmother always slept with a gun under her pillow whenever Mathew went out of town for work. One day a thief entered her bedroom. She pointed her gun at him and made him go under the bed and stay there until morning when she released him with the warning that if her husband heard about it, he would shoot him. I don't know if this was true, but things were raw back then. She was a brave woman. A street in Richmond Town in Bangalore is named Clapham Street.

A new sign erected for Clapham Street in Bangalore.

My family spent many happy times in Bangalore. My mother especially remembers living here and my grandparents and great-grandparents lived in this city. My mother often talked about the military parades on South Parade Road renamed Mahatma Gandhi (MG) Road in 1948.

76

Extended family taken in Bangalore in 1948 with my grandmother, my mother and myself, baby sister Jenny and Margo further down with aunts and friends.

MADRAS (CHENNAI)

My father, Stephen Joseph William Chase, was born in Katpadi, about two hours by train from Madras. Dad knew all the railways stops: Arcot, Arakkonam, Tiruvallur, Poonamalee, Kanchipuram. Vellore is a city known for the Christian Medical College and Hospital founded by Ida Scudder. Vellore now encompasses Katpadi, but it was another train stop on the way to Madras. Later, my dad had some land in Katpadi with a caretaker. Unfortunately, my mother also sent our dogs away to look after the property, but they were attacked and killed by the wild jackals. (Needless to say, she does not remember this part of the story.)

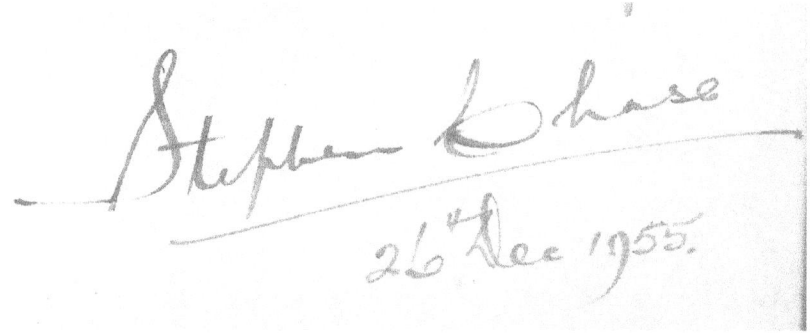

My dad's signature was distinctive, coming from his early days using copperplate lettering with pen and ink to write entries in the bank ledgers.

My paternal grandmother, my great-grandparents and their parents were born in Madras or Katpadi and lived there for over one hundred years. My grandmother remembered a great flood that enveloped the city of Madras. She said this flood only came once every hundred years. My cousin, Dorothea, built her house up high because she knew this story. She told me that when the flood came, many of the Anglo-Indians still living in that area of Poonamalee came to stay on her veranda above the flood waters.

My dad started working for the Imperial Bank on Mount Road as a clerk when he was eighteen, but we returned to Madras in 1945, just after the Second World War ended. At first, we stayed in a flat over Wilfred Pereira's Chemist Shop in Vepery, across from the clock tower. Then we moved to the Harbor View Hotel by First Line Beach, closer to the Head Office of the bank. It was around this time that I remember fishing off the dock at the harbor with my dad. It was shiny with the silicate mica minerals that were exported via ship from that harbor. We caught a big bucket of fish—lovely silverbelly fish called karapodi—but then Dad decided we should go for a walk. When we got back, the crows and seagulls had stolen all our fish!

Every evening, my mother would get us dressed up to walk down to the end of the lane to meet my dad after work. We spent the day in the hotel room and on the balcony, joining the other hotel guests for lunch. There was a kindly Chinese gentleman who would go out in a rickshaw and there were two British soldiers. One day, the two soldiers got drunk and started talking to my mother. When they found out she had a six-month-old baby asleep in her crib upstairs, they insisted on coming upstairs, carrying me on their shoulders, to look at the baby with my now terrified mother, who was only in her twenties at the time. Fortunately, my sister was still fast asleep and very cute, and they left quietly. My mother would take Margo and me on a bus to look for a place for us to live more permanently. She had a friend named Mrs. Shelby who helped us with tips, and we would spend the day following leads until we eventually found a flat which was a quarter of an old grand house in Vepery.

The house at 2/3 Ritherdon Lane (now Church Street) in Madras.

Originally a mansion, it had been cut up into apartments to house more than one family. My sister, Margo, was around two years old when she walked through a window (the only egress onto the deck) on to the hot cement and burned her little feet. All the windows had iron bars and we would loosen a bar to make the deck accessible. Margo also climbed the wood-apple tree with us when she was about three years old. I loved to crack those wood apples and eat the fruit with brown sugar. This large branching tree was by the front gate and a huge black ant bit her finger, taking a little chunk out of it while she screamed and screamed. I wonder if she still has a little scar.

We moved downstairs to a larger part of the house after a few months. It was while we lived at 2/3 Ritherdon Lane, that my dad was promoted to become a senior officer in the bank. He came home one day honking his horn all the way from the gate to the back of the house where he parked. We all ran out to find out the news. When he got his raise, he called everyone who worked in the house, including us children, to line up and he gave us all bonuses and pocket money, a gratefulness gesture that we all shared.

My sister Margo and I being taken to school in Madras.

There was a huge Asoka tree growing near this house. My dad built a long swing with a tire and rope from one of the strong branches. As a kid, I would climb up into the tree to sit in its cool shade and watch the long wavy leaves shake. Trees like these have all been chopped down in Chennai and I can only find miniature Asoka trees there now. My aunt, who later lived upstairs, callously said she was glad to see more light fill her apartment instead of the darkness the tree threw on her place.

I can never forget that first Independence Day in Madras in 1947. Dad took us in his Ford V8 automobile to see the city, Madras also always known as Chennai, which was all lit up for the celebrations. Of all those grand buildings, many gone now, Rippon Building, the Indo-Saracen Imperial Bank building, the High Courts were lighted up. A great-grand ancestor (a DeBeaux) was a barrister at the High Courts, and a statue of him was erected therein, although I have never been able to find it with all the restrictions in place for wandering about the courts. People walked in the streets chanting "Jai Hind, Jai Hind." Victory to India! I was a small child, but I remember the strength and vigor of that night. It thrilled me to my soul. I was not only a child of the Raj. I was Indian. Although an American citizen now, I still feel a daughter of India.

My littlest sister, Jennifer, was born in Madras in 1948, after Independence. Our family had a long sojourn in Madras, with a brief stop in Calcutta in between. We lived in the house on Ritherdon Lane where we had cows, rabbits, chickens (and turkeys near Christmas), a tortoise and, now and then, a dog for several years. One of the upstairs apartments was later occupied by my Uncle Len, his wife Aunty Daphne and their son Barry whose full name was Barrington Wayne Shepherd.

There is a small godown in the back, which is, sadly, lived in now and still has no electricity. We had a little godown, at one end, in the back of our quarters, where we stored things. It had no lights, so it was a scary place for us as children. We had a wooden rocking horse in the children's bedroom when we lived there that was so big that three of us could happily sit on it and rock back and forth. Sometimes my dad would sit on it and take one of us for a ride. We had some space in the back of the house where he had built a shed for three cows. My mother would sterilize the milk by parboiling and putting the milk in bottles to sell to a few neighbors. We had good clean tuberculosis-free milk and fresh eggs from the chickens. We had some pet bunnies, and they had their own shed, too. About once a month, a cart would come by with hay rolled in braids about twelve feet long that we would purchase and store in a garage next to the sheds. We would also buy nungoos in season from the travelling vendors. Those shiny ice-apples were so delicious on a hot day, the secret juice in the middle and tasty flesh around.

After we returned from Calcutta, we lived on Spur Tank Road, not far from a Tuberculosis Hospital with a domed roof. Rumor had it that the patients were given gold dust to eat to help them overcome the disease. We used to play in the field on one side of our house. There were huge tubes meant to be buried for water or sewage, but the project was never finished. The Couum River was opposite, far enough away from the blocked entry to the sea that it smelled like a normal river.

I took to pretending I was a javelin thrower like my aunt Audrey had been. I took up a crowbar (which is a long iron bar with a sharpened end that maybe looked like a crow's beak—it is used to pry open crates or sometimes to break into places). I used to throw it as far as I could on one side of the house near the garage. At this place I played at different times with my aunt Honie, our cook Alice's daughter Anthonyama and the boy upstairs, Pratap. This was one game that Pratap liked to play with me but one day, I had a premonition

Pen & Ink drawing by my dad -
State Bank of India Madras 1920s.

that I would kill one of the smaller children and stopped playing at javelin right then and went back to climbing the trees and making pretend curries. There was a stream at the end of the property from which we could hear frogs croaking at night and watch the gelatinous frog eggs floating along and turn into tadpoles and grow legs.

My dad had chickens here, too, which he insisted I learn to feed although I was terrified of them. I had a favorite who I named Cocky.

He was the lowest on the pecking order and I longed to rescue him and keep him as my pet, but my dad said: "No, the chickens will just pick another chicken to peck and soon all of them will die." I thought they would have more sense than that but soon poor little Cocky died and I cried for him. I buried him under the huge fig tree that grew by the chicken pen and carved his name on its trunk. I was never in tune with the ruthlessness of nature.

A drawing by my dad, probably in the 1930s.

This new place in Madras was like a townhouse with an apartment upstairs and another below. We lived upstairs for a while until my dad persuaded the people downstairs to move upstairs, which they preferred, and we moved down. There were eight bougainvillea bushes each with a different colored flower and a couple hybrid with two colors. Dad then grew papaya trees in a grove and had those chickens. A Gurkha guard was hired to patrol the area and keep thieves out, but he used to bang his stick on the walls all night, keeping my dad up. One day, Dad told him in no uncertain terms that he was to do a quieter patrol. After that, the neighborhood was never sure they were being protected and wondered if the so-called guard had taken to sleeping instead. We had a male staff person who helped in the house. An old lady would sit on a rock outside our gate and wait for him to get off work and bully him to go to the prostitutes that she represented. Unfortunately, he succumbed one night and contracted a venereal disease, and he could not work for us anymore.

My parents went on a vacation to England for three months and my grandmother, my dad's mother Adelaide, came to stay with us. She did not like the fans, so the heat really got to us, and I got a bad case of boils. By the age of twelve, I was the house mechanic. I could fix the electric coil stoves and the pump for the well.

It wasn't until the 1960s that my dad was transferred back to

Madras, and we lived at Red Craig, a beautiful mansion built around 1800. We found it on a map of 1850. It is mentioned in the Vestiges of Old Madras 1640-1800 (Indian Record Series) 4 vols on page 535 as being on College Road. It was a grand old house with large bedrooms and dressing rooms. The dining room and living room were like ballrooms. There was an eight-foot high three-part solid coromandel screen that stood on its own in the dining room, covering the entrance to the pantry and kitchen. The kitchens in those old colonial houses were built apart from the house to keep the smoke from the wood burning fuel and the aroma of spices from permeating the house. Coriander, cumin, and turmeric with a pinch of asafetida create a deep sweet aroma when they are fried with onions and tomatoes to make a curry base.

The kitchen was also the domain of the men who worked for the house and not a place that I, as a girl child and then a young woman, was allowed to hang out. Finally, when I was in college, my mother allowed me to use the kitchen to experiment with some recipes, but only in the afternoon while the cook and his helpers were out on a siesta break.

Photo of our family taken at Red Craig in 1962

In some of the homes we lived in like this one, my mother had her own electric kitchen in the house next to the storeroom where she locked the dry goods—sugar, tea, rice, dals, beans, and spices. Many spices had to be ground for a curry, each one different and unique to each dish. Green and black cardamom, black mustard and fenugreek were added to garlic, ginger, and fresh green ingredients such as coriander leaves and fresh coconut and made into a paste on a grinding stone. Chilies were added according to taste, either green or dried. Chilies are a fairly new ingredient, introduced to India from South America in the sixteenth century. Many ancient cuisines in India do not use hot chilies, or even tomatoes, which were also originally imported.

This mansion in Madras, Red Craig, had a tamarind grove on one side of the house that filled with delightful, sweet-sour tamarinds but it was contracted out. The large verandas at Red Craig were perfect for entertaining. My uncle Len would come and spend the day sometimes, telling jokes and smoking while we drank orange crush and embroidered linens. During exam months—the hot summer months —I studied on the veranda until the early hours of the mornings. The in-house Gurkha guard paced the grounds while I studied, and my little dog, Dinky, kept me company until around 2 AM when he finally got restless and barked to get me to stop and go to bed. It was then that the guard made his last round.

"Red Craig" taken from the side. This house has been demolished.

When I lived with the Pereira's during my college years in Madras (before my dad was transferred back), we stayed up late studying, too. We could watch students on all the rooftops studying, but when one student gave up, usually around two or three o'clock in the morning, and switched off his or her lights then all the students would also give up and go to bed. Kids would fly their kites from the rooftops, having kite fights and competing to be highest until dusk before the serious college students started studying.

I loved to be in a hurricane in Madras, out on a balcony and getting soaked by the rain. A hurricane is so exhilarating. Watching the big trees swaying, especially the palms, was magical. It was sad if the storms wreaked damage disturbing terra ferma. I loved to watch the ocean from the balcony verandas when I stayed at Queen Mary's College, opposite the sands of the third-widest beach in the world. The changing colors and the swells were a symmetry that brought all that was peaceful to my heart. We studied all over the college grounds. I could get a newspaper to put down to keep out the cold and damp from the cement floor of a veranda and sit and study like that for hours. Sometimes I would take the train up to Bangalore to visit my family when they were there, and I was in Madras. I would take a footlocker with me and sit on it, then sleep on it in the third-class compartment overnight, afraid to be in first class where all the robberies happened. I also stayed at the YWCA for a while in the students' quarters. I would pay the mali (gardener) to get me one bucket of hot water to have a bath. He would heat this on a wood fire outdoors. Often, I would only get half a bucket because his bucket had a hole. I was given a room with two other students, one of whom had her Hindu gods displayed on the wall above my bed. The first month I was continually woken up at night with "something" jumping on me. Convinced they were the spirits of the revered gods who were angry with me for setting up house in their domain, I asked her to move them over. This was an all-day ceremony, but she complied. Now, when I think of it, it was probably only squirrels jumping in and out of an open window.

When we lived at Red Craig, there was an immense mansion

further down the road in an open field. It lay abandoned for many years. I was told it was owned by a Muslim family who had fled to Pakistan during partition and were all murdered on the trains at the borders. This is a very sad legacy of the division of India at Independence. The house remained abandoned for many, many years but eventually the city took it over and built police barracks on the land.

The font at St. Mary's Church in Fort St. George in Madra

My dad spent many days at St. Mary's Church in Fort St. George looking through the records to find information about our family. I think he found it difficult during those pre-digital days, but he told me he found an ancestral woman who had the last name Cherry and he assumed this was the Indian surname Cherian. We don't know for sure.

When I lived at the YWCA, I attended the impressive Scott's Kirk about a mile down the road. It's beautiful round theatre, doors opened on all sides, and its enormous steeple could be seen from all over Madras.

I found records of my great grandmother, Jane DeBeaux's, marriage there and later her grave in Bangalore. My Uncle Len told me that she came from a French ship building family in Normandy. I have visited the beautiful city of Normandy. Historically, Normandy often slipped between the British and French rule. It is on the ocean and played a big part in D-Day in 1944. There are graves of young men from many countries in Normandy—British, American, French, Polish, German, Indian—all in their early twenties. When I was in Normandy we got lost and I saw a woman gardening outside. I got out of the car and asked her in my limited French where we could find an international graveyard. She answered in Spanish, which I don't know, and we ended up speaking in English. She was a British war widow, still taking care of the soldiers' graves—sons, brothers, fathers, husbands, and lovers.

Ancestors in the Chase family lived in an area in Madras known as Chinglepet. It was named for the father of the Naik of Chinglepet Chennapa and the area around this village became known as Chennapatanam, shortened to Chennai, the current name of the city of Madras. Around 1687, the British Army paid soldiers who married local women a stipend, probably to have them settle down and live a quieter married life. My dad often quoted a book called The History of Madras, which he said told of how the British imported a shipload of English women to help the soldiers marry their own kind, but many years later it was found that many of these women remained "old maids" because the soldiers preferred the local women.

My cousin Ruth Croft standing at our great-great grandmother Jane DeBeaux' grave at Hosur Cemetery in Bangalore in 2000.

Thus, the Anglo-Indian traditions started with the spices, the beauty, and the ability to translate of the women where they remained for many years.

It was in Madras that my grandmother Adelaide and my Aunty Thelma (Uncle Richard Chase's wife) and my Aunty Eunice (Dad's sister) would make the most delicious vindaloo curries. I still remember the flavor and depth of this curry and I try to recreate its richness.

GOA

Although we never lived there, I have many good memories of visiting Goa (later in life) and staying in the city of Colva. My Aunt Honie (my mother's sister from the Shepherd/Lilywhite line) and my cousins went there regularly. I wrote to friends about one of my visits: "Yesterday we spent the day on the beach in Colva, in front of Jack Rodriquez' thatched restaurant Sucarina. We found a lounge chair covered in sarongs and enjoyed the warm sunshine. Rodriquez had built a twenty-foot open hut for all of us to take cover. The ocean was calm, and we began the process of removing the dark circles from under our eyes and the furrows in our brows. The aches and pains in our bodies from the thirty-hour flight via Mumbai from America slowly dissipated. Dodging the waves and the breakers, watching the fishermen come in early before dawn and the fisherwomen carrying away baskets of fresh fish was our work for the day. Eating tandoori pomfret fish, masala mackerel, stuffed parottas, fresh coconut filled pancakes with lime and honey and a banana lassi or Kingfisher beer, chicken tikka masala or Desai Chinese—all part of the day's feasting. Not to forget the fresh chili and tomato omelets for breakfast with chai (or coffee with chicory). Seductions all around: Sharifi's gold shop, the expatriate Kashmiri stalls, the church bells peeling at dawn along with the roosters crowing. Catching up with my first cousins and my aunt and all their families. The Prime Minister visiting Goa, staying at the upscale Taj Exotica hotel down the way. His helicopters buzzed the beach, annoyingly. There is one parasail attracting hordes of Indian tourists further up. We wish him God-speed to whichever spoiled beach he came from and to the speed boat that was frightening the fish which are essential to the Goan economy. Foreign tourists here are

International—many British, others from Poland, Russia, Germany, France. We can hear many languages on the beach. Today is another balmy day with a light breeze off the Indian Ocean where you can stay in the water until your fingers wrinkle, and you need to drink fresh coconut water or lie in the bright sun to burn lightly. Such a life!" — Sunday, December 29, 2002. Colva.

5

FAMOUS PEOPLE: ANGLO-INDIANS AND ALLIES

There is plenty of information on the Internet about our Anglo-Indian history and people of note. I will write, rather, something about my own experiences and, contextually, about Anglo-Indians in India and abroad. History plays a part.

It was in those last lingering days after the Raj had ended, its memories fresh in my mind, that I heard Pundit Nehru speak. Soon after Independence, Anglo-Indians were eager to know what the future of India would look like—if it could be foretold. We were experiencing the embers waiting for the phoenix to arise.

I took our Indian-made blue and white Standard Triumph automobile and drove out to a large open maidan field on the outskirts of Madras, where Nehru was scheduled to speak. A huge crowd of several thousand people had gathered. Nehru was high up on a platform and people, mostly men, stood in the audience. He spoke in his flawless Cambridge accent, his mellifluous voice charged with sincerity and grounded in the belief of freedom for all. His speech was translated into Tamil, sentence by sentence and phrase by phrase. I admired Gandhi, Nehru, Nehru's sister Madame Vijaya Lakshmi Pandit and Indira Gandhi, Nehru's daughter. Jawaharlal Nehru was the Prime Minister of India and Madame Pandit was president of the

United Nations General Assembly. Indira Gandhi was yet to become Prime Minister.

Me with my dog Dinky and our Studebaker, before we bought the Triumph, 1962.

I parked the car right behind the stage, as this was before the days of heightened security. I got out and stood by my car. No one bothered me. I wore a blue polka-dot dress with a starched petticoat under it. There was not the slightest breeze, the air was crisp. Nehru spoke for an hour and we were all silent, listening. When he concluded and the thunderous applause began, I started up the engine and drove away before the crowd started to disperse. I was one of the few women in Madras who drove a car and the traffic was manageable. I told nobody at home where I was going. Those were the days when the Nehru dynasty was in its infancy, still firing up the country with a strong sense of nationalism. Sadly, it was at this venue, many years later, that Nehru's grandson Rajiv was blown to pieces by a suicide bomber. Indira Gandhi was also assassinated by one of her own Sikh guards after she had ordered an armed search for weapons inside the Golden Temple in Amritsar. But on that day, I was enthralled by our first Prime Minister, Jawaharlal Nehru.

There were so-called Englishmen who were actually Anglo-Indians. There were Anglo-Indians who claimed they were not Indian, and Indians who claimed they were Anglo-Indian. The politics of the day, with prejudices evidenced in job security and housing, altered the biographies and histories of many families. Because of their long footprint many British families lived in India for generations. Sometimes their children would be sent to England for schooling or to stay with relatives. Until the Raj really ended, these families never considered spending their entire lives in that country they called "home" because their hearts and minds were deeply in India. I was recently pleasantly surprised to find out that a family I thought was so English had lived in India for three generations on both sides of the family and some had married Anglo-Indians. It happened.

Rudyard Kipling, who received the Nobel Prize for Literature in 1907, would have been considered an Anglo-Indian in the British sense. He was born in Bombay in 1865 when his father, Lockwood Kipling, was head of the Jamsetjee Jeejeebhoy School of Arts. Rudyard was educated in England and then, naturally, returned to India where he was a journalist. Kipling wrote many of his fictional works and poetry in India, such as The Ballad of East and West, which he wrote in 1889. The first line of this poem is often quoted, but Kipling also wrote that "there is neither East nor West", a fact exemplified and understood by the Anglo-Indian. Kipling's father, also later the curator of the Lahore Museum, designed gas lamps for the durbar for Lord Lytton in India in 1876. The durbar was an elaborate pageant to commemorate Lord Lytton's installment as Governor General and Viceroy to India. British families in India just could not get India out of their blood. Their histories were mixed with ours, intertwined.

Lord and Lady Lytton's sons both married women whose parents had lived in India and who had lived there themselves as children. Victor Lytton was made Governor of Bengal and returned to Calcutta's government house where he had played as a child. Edwin Lutyens, who married Emily Lytton, designed the Vice-Regal Palace, in Delhi, in 1912.

A similar story is told of the Mountbattens, who ended the Raj at Independence. Lord Mountbatten was the last Viceroy and Governor

General of India. When he visited the Nilgiris in his official capacity, several of us school children, boarders at Lushington Hall and Clifton Grange, managed to smuggle our autograph books into Government House which was at the top of the hill of the formal public botanical gardens in Ooty. We got signatures to keep as a memory. Even Princess Diana is said to have had a great-great-grandmother who was an Anglo-Indian ancestor in Bombay. We are the children of the children of the children of the Raj.

On January 1, 1877, Queen Victoria was declared Empress of India. This was the beginning of the high Raj period when the massed military bands played *God Save the Queen*. The Raj lasted less than a century until 1947, outlasting Queen Victoria. The Raj spirit of optimism and English and European cultural leanings started much earlier and continued afterwards. Winnowing the good from the ugly, Anglo-Indians tended to fend for themselves as best they could in that colonial era of inequity.

Family at the beach in 1949. L-R Adults—Daphne, Len, my mother. Children—Margo, Barry, myself and Jenny.

On my maternal side, stories persist of a cousin who was lady-in-waiting to Queen Victoria. She wrote of life in the palace in exchange for letters from India. Her letters were lost when they were in the possession of the Thipthorpe cousins, according to my mother. On a genealogy list, I found another cousin, Ruth, with our family names (Lilywhite and Clapham) and the same lady-in-waiting story. This has led to successful discoveries of my mother's first cousins in Bombay, her maternal grandfather Patrick Lilywhite's progeny. These cousins spell their name slightly differently.

Felicity Kendal, whose parents had a travelling theater company, grew up touring India. She attended several Catholic schools around the country. Felicity played Shakespearean roles at a young age. I saw the *Merchant of Venice* performed at a school in Madras. I also saw a beautiful rendition of the *Dance of Seven Veils* from *Salome* by Richard Strauss then. Felicity Kendal went to England and became well known in the television series of The Good Life—a theme she probably learned as a child from the Anglo-Indian belief in the good life. Her sister married into an Indian movie-star family and stayed on.

India, the country of fabled peacock thrones and the Kohinoor diamond, carries its brilliant secrets from before Shah Jehan to beyond Victoria Regis. Both high society and the lowlife of British-Indian history were often recorded in journals, watercolors, and black and white photographs. Not everyone in the Raj was a viceroy or vicereine surrounded by male and female servants serving hot tea and pulling large fans called punkas to create a breeze in the oppressive heat. There were thousands of ordinary soldiers, civil servants, apothecaries, drummers and their wives and families who also lived during the Raj. There was a disparity in fortunes between the tea plantation owner and the engine driver, although both took great pride in their work. The engine driver probably had more recognition and respect in the Anglo-Indian populated railways. However low on the power structure totem pole, in however small a barracks or railway quarters, still there would be a china teacup, a copy of a Shakespeare play and the tinkling sounds of a spinet piano playing a scale or two or a popular song of the times. You would know that the Raj lived on in the best of ways, negating colonialism, and imperialism. The soul of the Anglo-Indian glowed even when nothing but embers remained. Prejudice, racial profiling and stereotyping common in India was keenly felt yet did not deter the Anglo-Indian from enjoying life.

On one visit, I met a lady who lived in a godown in the back of the house on Ritherdon Lane where we had lived in the 1940s. She said she was the aunt of Engelbert Humperdinck, the famous British singer whose roots are in Madras. Although he often denied these early beginnings, he has admitted them more recently. His Anglo-Indian name was Arnold George Dorsey. The Dorseys were a family my father knew in his youth in Madras. Arnold (aka Engelbert) has made millions upon millions of dollars with his mellifluous, romantic voice. I hope he is helping less fortunate and gifted Anglo-Indians now. Cliff Richards is another favorite singer who made it big in England. He was born Harry Rodger Webb in Lucknow.

In the evenings in India, a few people might gather while some talented family member played the piano and sang along to songs like, *She'll Be Coming 'Round the Mountain* or *The Donkey Serenade*. In Calcutta, you could hear the bagpipers playing old songs like Danny Boy and songs from the First World War. It was the way of the Raj and Anglo-Indians to always put a positive spin on life.

In the *Lay of the last Minstrel*, Sir Walter Scott wrote:

Breathes there the man with soul so dead
Who never to himself hath said,
This is my own, my native land!
Whose heart hath ne'er within him burned,
As home his footsteps he hath turned
From wandering on a foreign strand!

This poem, which we memorized as children in India, often left us wondering: What foreign strand? As thousands of British and Anglo-Indians later found on making their homes in England after Independence, India was home. India is our "native land." There was no place more foreign to us than Britain, Canada, Australia, or America—the countries to which we dispersed in our diaspora—but home we made it. We are, in fact, the offspring of the Raj and of India. Our children are British, Canadian, Australian, or American with strong Anglo-Indian roots.

When I was in those disciplined Anglo-Indian schools, we

memorized poems from *Palgrave's Golden Treasury of the best Songs and Lyrical Poems in the English Language* (published in 1861 and 1912). We visualized the Lake District of Wordsworth's "I wander'd lonely as a cloud…" and the icy waters of Lochgyle in the Hebrides in *Lord Ullin's Daughter*. Our own Anglo-Indian poet said it better. Henry Louis Vivian Derozio (1807-1831) wrote in *The Harp of India*:

But if thy notes divine may be by mortal wakened once again,
Harp of my country, let me strike the strain!

6

AN ODE TO MY UNCLE LEN
A GENTLEMAN

In those sultry days in India, we were pleased when my Uncle Len visited for the day. It was entirely up to him when he arrived and how long he stayed, but he always stayed for lunch. He smoked his Marlborough cigarettes as we sat on the veranda and entertained him—or rather, he us—for hours and hours. He was spending time with my mother, his older sister by a few years. He was ambitious and bright and loved himself no end. This was alright, we loved and adored him, too. He became the general manager of Binny Mills, known as Binny's (Buckingham and Carnatic Mills) in Madras and Bangalore, where he oversaw a manufacturing and office staff of four thousand. Before he started at Binny's, before anyone had attempted divorce, before anyone had died, he was there to while away the day with the international news, good stories, and jokes.

Len was born in Wellington in the Nilgiri Hills, like my mother and several siblings when the family was living in the army quarters there. He was baptized at St. George's Church of England. He married Daphne Fitzgerald in Bangalore and they honeymooned at the Krishna Raja Sagara dam (KRS). They stayed at the Brindavan Hotel on the edge of the beautiful Brindavan gardens, which were filled with flowering plants and lighted fountains that danced to music in the evenings. It was a beautiful and romantic place, built originally by Krishna Raja Wadiyar IV the maharaja of Mysore in 1931. Over the years the availability of electricity here seems to have dwindled. When I visited a few years ago there was only two hours of the show, with thousands of people crossing the dam to get to the top of the garden before the music began and the fountains started to flow. Len and Daph had a record player and would play Nat King Cole's *Unforgettable* over and over again. How can I forget those days?

My mother (in the middle) with her brother Len and her sister Honie (Doris)
holding up their dosais at Ulla's in Bangalore in 2000.

We sat on that long wide veranda at Red Craig in Madras, my mother, my sisters and I, with our embroidery. I was particularly good with feather stich and satin stich, but I abhorred cross stich, which my sister loved and still does. We sat and listened and laughed and embroidered flowers on pillowcases, thinking it was the most natural occupation in the world. The staff brought cold orange crush in little glasses on a silver tray. When the cook had fixed everything in the outside kitchen, he would call us to lunch.

My Uncle Leonard David Shepherd taken by me in 1984

Uncle Len would pass a mirror and say to us "Don't I look good? You have to admit I look good, don't you?" He was vanity personified, but we indulged him. He talked about the world as if it was such a small place, bringing in politics and news of change everywhere. We discussed the monumental changes occurring in the world after the

Second World War. Independence was not just in India, but also for Pakistan and countries in Africa, the Middle East and Asia. Countries changed their names. He read the Blitz newspaper which was iconoclastic and investigative that some thought was communist. The world came alive as we talked. Nehru was Prime Minister, and although Mahatma Gandhi had been assassinated, the nascent independent India seemed filled with hope and intention. Good people were at the helm and graft and bribery and corruption were not paramount behaviors. The prevalent thinking was that the "India for Indians" philosophy would crowd Anglo-Indians out of employment and empowerment. The idea that we could "return" to the West after a quasi-heritage of 300 to 500 years and blend unnoticed into an almost foreign culture was strangely popular—and many tried. Over seventy years later we are still searching for those Indian roots deep in our souls and that Indian sun to warm our hearts and bones. Uncle Len never left India.

He often recalled the days when he walked from Burma to India at the end of the War. He was in the British Indian Army but because of his training at Bishop Cottons School, he served on the administrative side. He told us of the Japanese bombers flying over cities in Burma, killing people who ran out into the streets to watch. His older brothers, Harry Roslyn and Eddie, had been taken into the army while still in their teens and fought in different locations. After the war, Eddie was honored with a Military Medal from King George VI for his heroism at Dunkirk. The discipline my Uncle Len got from his army days showed up in many little ways. His insistence on flat ironed sheets on his bed made up with hospital corners, was one.

Their father, Harry Shepherd, had been transferred to Wellington by his regiment. It would be left to my grandmother to organize the house and children and follow him to each assignment. Thus, he was moved from Belgaum to Bangalore and to Wellington. After this move the regiment was ordered back to England, but many, many British soldiers did not want to return to their own country, perhaps remembering the cold and the coal-burning sooty air. My grandfather was one of many who found jobs at the nearby Armory in Aravankadu overseeing the guns and artillery being securely kept there. After he retired from the army my grandfather decided to stay on. There was no school in the cordite factory grounds, so the children were taken to local English schools in the area by car—at that time it was the Tin Lizzy, a Model T.

Uncle Len's wife, my Aunty Daphne, was a generous, beautiful woman who loved to play songs and while the evenings away listening to Nat King Cole: "Mona Lisa, Mona Lisa…you're so like the lady with the mystic smile…" When I was in college at Queen Mary's in Madras, she would have me over for dinner. It would be saved in the meat-safe, a cupboard with mesh doors. She did not have a refrigerator. She was very kind to me. It was a sadness that broke their hearts when my cousin, their son Barry, died in a lorry accident. They split up and Uncle Len married a beautiful young widow, Pam and they had Diedre and Sean, my good cousins.

Uncle Len stayed on in India even after our immediate families left—to America, Canada, Australia, New Zealand and even Kuwait. How could we ever have known it would be like this? But, in those transformative days in India, on that wide veranda, we were living the embers of the Raj life. Leonard David Lawrence Shepherd was still living in Bangalore in his 90s. He died there in 2021 a month before

Len, Daphne, and Barry taken around 1950.

his 97th birthday. I will always miss him, my precious Uncle Len who shaped some of my most formative years. As Nat King Cole sang my Uncle Len was:

Unforgettable
In every way,
And forever more
That's how you'll stay.

7

ANGLO-INDIAN WOMEN WHO INFLUENCED ME

(FEMME FENG SHUI)

My dad liked to visit old ladies. He kept tabs on them over the years. I often accompanied him on these visits. One of these women, Mrs. Clara Dunhill gave me an antique needle case, which I still have. It was very old, even then. She was married to a much older man whom she did not love (so I was told), but she became an influential woman. I loved to visit her house, filled with antiques, while she and my dad chatted over the formality of tea. She was very influential and called her friend, Mr. Rollandson, to ask him to give my dad a job at the bank. I think she was 80 when my dad was only 30. I remember visiting her home with my dad.

My dad helped many ladies in his job, including the famous Lady Stow. They liked his proficiency with English, accounting, and his meticulous attention to detail. My mother said that his peon came to the house to deliver some mail and told her, "Ma, you must see master's table with all the ladies around it, like a film star he is!"

My dad's cousin, Edna, who had been married to a man she also did not love, arranged marriages were not uncommon in those days. She had some children when she was younger, not all of whom survived. I remember my dad telling me that she had had twins and a son. She suffered blindness in her old age. Dad and I visited her when she lived in Austin Town in Bangalore. I keep in touch with her great-grandchildren on social media.

Lady Stokes on her veranda in the 1930s.

Another old lady, one who my dad did not know, lived at Montauban in Ooty. I visited her during a health-related holiday in Ooty around 1949, along with my mother and sisters. My mother had become weak with low blood pressure after the birth of my sister and had been advised to get away from the heat of Madras. This lady had the most exquisite dolls and gave me a porcelain doll with blue eyes, which I treasured until I was sent to boarding school. My mother gave it away while I was gone, and I imagine some ayah's granddaughter is still playing with it more than half a century later; or it may have another life in a china cabinet behind a prized obsolete camera and a Chinese bowl; or perhaps she's dressed in silk and gold and playing the role of the Madonna at some small roadside church. Who knows?

ARRANMORE HOUSE,
OOTACAMUND,
S. INDIA.

19 . 4 . 43.

Dear Mr Chase,

beg my congratulations on your well deserved promotion, which I was so glad to hear about from Mr Rao.

It is nice to know that your hard work has been recognised & I hope you will go up rapidly on the ladder of success!

With kindest regards to your wife & yourself. Yours sincerely

Violet Stow

Arranmore House was probably on the property of the Arranmore Palace which was built by the Maharajah of Jodhpur and is now a Government guest house.

Then there was Mrs. Copley, whom my dad and I visited when I was very young. She lived near the market in Ooty, in a tiny flat with a bird in a cage. I don't remember my mother coming along, but she told me that this lady had been her grandmother's friend. I wonder what happened to her.

Importantly, there was my grandmother, Adelaide née Blanche, who had the best stories to tell. There was one about her cousin who was buried alive. Although believed to be dead, she had been in a coma. Grandma heard the rap, tap, tap on the coffin from inside the lid, but no one paid her any mind, and the woman was buried as scheduled. Grandma had three children: my Uncle Richard (the violinist); my Aunty Eunice (the fearless) and my dad, Stephen Joseph William Chase (the banker, preacher, father, husband, and son). Her second husband was twenty years her junior. We didn't talk much of him. He died long before her of Kala-azar (black fever) and left her a pension which she received the rest of her life. My dad supplemented both my grandmothers' incomes as they got older, even my mother's parents who lived in England. It was his filial duty and he stepped up to it. My grandmother, Adelaide, always wore a locket with a picture on each side—one of her first husband, my grandfather Albert, and the other of her second husband, Harry. I notice that I sit the way she did with one knee cocked to the side. I guess I inherited some of her genes.

I never met my great aunt Dr. Esther Chase, one of my dad's favorites. She ran her medical practice out of the big house that is now the YWCA International Guest House compound on Poonamallee High Road in Chennai. I do not know whether she owned or rented, the property, but when I lived at the YWCA while I was in college, the secretary told me that she had seen my great aunt's name on the deed and she showed it to me. It was a grand old house with big trees and a beautiful lake on the property. As a child, we would often go to these gardens to play by the pond, many years after Dr. Esther was gone. She was a physician for the Zenana Mission and treated women who were in seclusion.

At the age of thirty, Dr. Chase decided that she would not be getting married and went to England where she got her medical degree. She practiced medicine by visiting the women who were in purdah, who were kept within their homes and courtyards. Because of cultural or religious taboos, these women were not allowed to mix with men or to be seen by a male physician. Later, she went to work on the Andaman Islands where she provided her medical services in a dedicated way.

The main house at the YWCA on Poonamalee High Road in Madras.

Dr. Esther Chase adopted her brother's children and raised them in this house on Poonamallee High Road. She determined the day of her own death when the oldest boy was visiting from England. "Lord, take me now," she prayed as she paced the house. He stayed long enough to bury her in Bangalore. She lives on in the memories of her family passed down through the generations. My dad was greatly influenced by her. He said when he went to church with her, she would ask him if he was a coward. When he answered in the negative, she would lead him with her to sit in the front of the church. My dad admired her and often talked of her. He had an English dictionary that she had given him, and he would sign it every ten years in her memory.

I had the names of four of these women written on pieces of paper and stuck up in the four corners of my office at home. It was a Feng Shui suggestion that I had read about, to give me inspiration—and this they did. These women continue to inspire me. The women whose names were on my wall were: Mrs. Dunhill, Amy Chase, Mrs. Copland, and Dr Esther Chase.

Mercy Earlam, my dad's cousin who I think was Leda Chase's daughter.

Although many Anglo-Indians left India after Independence, some who stayed on were strong women who made great contributions to India and the remaining Anglo-Indians. Dr. Beatrix Xavier D'Souza is one of them. She has provided innumerable benefits to the community, including representing them in the legislature as a Member of Parliament. She was my English professor at Queen Mary's College when I was a student there.

The pervasive message is that Anglo-Indian women are the backbone of the community. With their recipes, their devotion to God and their unwavering loyalty to their children, they created examples that most of us will never be able to fully duplicate however hard we try.

A version of this chapter was published by CTR in *Women of Anglo-India; Tales and Memoirs* (2010) titled *Femme Feng Shui*

Note: Researching Mrs. Dunhill, I find that she or one of her ancestors belonged to the Fellowship of Baldwin's School in Bangalore that helped fund the school in its beginnings. Although she married into the Dunhill family, she continued its traditions. The name Dunhill is still known in Bangalore. A book about Helen E. Dunhill, a missionary who travelled the world with her mission to stop the flow of opium to India has been reproduced by Alfred S. Dyer, republished by Asbury Theological Seminary in 2020. Helen Dunhill states that her great-grandfather married a local woman and that she was also an Anglo-Indian in heritage.
https://issuu.com/asburytheologicalseminary/docs/
dyer__a._saunders_a_christian_daughter_of_india_nw

Dr. Esther Chase was a lay missionary before she became a doctor for the Zenana Mission. She was recommended by the Committee on Missionary Candidates for the Woman's Foreign Missionary Society in 1898 and joined the Baltimore Branch. This item is mentioned in The Christian Advocate, New York, 1898 volume 73. She was a lay missionary for the Vepery Tamil Mission (reported in the South India missionary report of 1885) for the Missionary Society of the Methodist Episcopal Church, Madras District. She also worked for the Girl's High School in Madras.

Amy Chase was my dad's cousin and someone he cared for in many ways, but she was a single woman and liked to travel and moved constantly. She suffered from fears and anxieties. She was creative, talented, and intellectual who had been jilted in love.

Feng Shui is a Chinese system and practice of arranging the pieces in living spaces to create balance with the natural world.

My Aunty Eunice (my dad's sister) with her husband, Dennis.

8

THE QUINTESSENTIAL ANGLO-INDIAN LADY

MY MOTHER

My mother, Phyllis Violet Isabel (Shepherd) Chase at 100 taken by my sister, Margo, in Brisbane, Australia.

Isabel is my mother, and therefore a person whom I can never really know and yet have known intimately since my birth. Her full name is Phyllis Violet Isabel Chase née Shepherd. The trajectory of her life and almost all its salient features are well known to me and to my family. But who is she, really, and what influenced her, making her flexible in some areas and totally rigid in others? Does the need to adapt and change make a person seek and cling to a safe mast to keep the ship of their life afloat? How did she manage a successful business that made her financially independent in her advancing years in Australia?

My mother was born on February 7, 1921, in a British military hospital in Wellington, in the Nilgiri hills of South India. She is now over one hundred years old. Her father, Harry Shepherd, was born in Norwich, England. At a young age (he falsified his age upwards) he joined the Norfolk Regiment and was sent to Mesopotamia where he fought the ancient Ottoman Empire with the British allies and to Europe to fight for England in World War I. The First Battalion of this famous regiment was stationed in India until the onset of World War II and was renamed the Royal Norfolk Regiment in 1935 after having been in existence for 250 years. Harry, my grandfather, went to India with his regiment and met my grandmother, Florence Grace Lilywhite, whose family had lived in India for generations.

My mother was one of nine siblings, the oldest girl and thus was given many responsibilities. Not too many, perhaps, because her aunt, affectionately called Natta, and her grandmother, Lilly, also lived with them and helped, along with various household staff who cooked, cleaned, and cared for the children.

My grandfather traded his Ford Model T in for a Chrysler when the new model came out. We have many amusing family stories about their driver, Arakaswamy. He was known to exchange the children's sandwiches for puffed rice. He drove them to school in Conoor, Ooty and other hill stations. At one point, my grandmother set up a boarding house in Ooty and took in paying guests to be near the schools.

My mother was very fond of her next to youngest sibling, Charlie, who died from diphtheria and complications of pneumonia at the tender age of two. He was buried in St. Thomas' church cemetery, and it is recorded at St. Stephen's Church in Ooty. My grandmother was ill and at the same hospital at the time. After sojourns in Belgaum, Bangalore and other areas in Karnataka, my grandfather retired as a sergeant major and decided to stay on in India. My mother attended several schools in the Nilgiris, including Breeks (now Hebron International School) in Ooty, Lovedale (where she was a boarder with her older brother when she was only six), Stanes School (where her grandmother worked as a matron) and St. Joseph's College in Coonoor (as a day student when she was young). Sometimes she remembers these schools in a different order or not at all. After the sad demise of her much-loved little brother, my grandmother moved down to Bangalore with the extended family, including her last baby girl, Honie Doris, for a warmer climate. My mother, occasionally, will tell me how she still feels the sadness late at night when she thinks of her brother Charlie. My grandfather continued to work in the Nilgiris to support the family.

Although my mother excelled in French and other subjects in school, she decided to curtail her studies and take a dressmaking course. She was accepted for a job as an assistant matron in one of the schools, following the profession of her grandmother who worked after the separation from her husband. My mother's grandfather, my great-grandfather, Patrick Lilywhite (whom she never knew) worked for the railways in Bombay for much of his life. In those days, details of such separations or a divorce were kept secret and not discussed in front of children, so my mother grew up not knowing her maternal grandfather. In fact, it was 80 years before we found her cousins via the Internet and held a reunion with them in the Mazagaon area, opposite the six-story-steepled Gloria Church, in Bombay. This church, Nossa Senhora de Gloria, was originally built by the Portuguese in 1632. It is opposite a market that has probably been there longer. At dusk, when you hear the church bells ring, you also hear the Muslim call to prayer.

Isabel, my mother, taught Sunday school at All Saints Church in Bangalore. This church is now a Heritage Building on Hosur Road where my uncle Len maintained a membership. It's lands and access are threatened by the new Metro. She then attended the Richmond Town Methodist Church. Later, she attended the Gospel Hall in Richmond Town, which was run by Dr. Marrett who also ran a free clinic. It was at the Gospel Hall that she met my father, Stephen Chase.

Isabel and Stephen had two tiered cakes at their wedding in 1939.

They married and moved all over India, wherever he was posted by his employer, the Imperial Bank of India—Bangalore, Colombo (Sri Lanka), Tellecherry, and Ellore. They lived on a houseboat in Ellore for four days each month on the Godavari River while my dad checked warehouses and physical stocks for the bank. I remember a time when my dad had to check the gold stock being held at a mine in Kolar Gold Fields. Heaps of potassium cyanide, used for some aspect of gold plating, were in locked rooms which we were allowed to see. Other cities they lived in were Calcutta, Allepey, Cochin, Hyderabad, (many have had their names changed since) and Madras. My mother never became a school matron and stayed at home to raise her children instead.

My parents wedding (L-R) my grandparents, best man Tom Axford and bridesmaid Isobel Pettigrew, and flower girls my mother's sisters Audrey and Gwen, 1939.

My mother was only 19 when she gave birth to me in Coimbatore. Of my siblings, Margo, was born in Ooty, Jenifer in Madras and Eric in Colombo, Sri Lanka. My mother was a supreme hostess and learned to cook delicacies and do embroidery. I have a few of her intricate cross-stitched tapestries in my home now. She designed and made her own clothes and often ours as well. I remember her wonderful chutneys, gooseberry and guava jams, and fruit salads. She made large quantities of this fruit salad sometimes to contribute to her charities. In Ooty during the War years, my dad taught her how to make leather handbags on her sewing machine and she had a small business. After the war, some years later, a lady pointed to a handbag she was still using and told me that my mother had made it.

My father took more and more challenging positions and when I was in college, he became the manager of the Bangalore Branch of what was by then, after India's Independence, the State Bank of India. We lived above the bank in a palatial suite on a six-acre park-like property with household staff provided by the bank, and our own cook and driver. We were often told how when my parents married, my dad had shown my mother the small accountant's home on the property and thought he may retire from there, but because of his persistence and the end of the Raj, they were able to live in the big house with the tennis courts and ebony staircase. Once a month they would have song services on the veranda of their home with over a hundred people in attendance. This was the house that was called Hopeville. My dad ended his career by retiring from Red Craig, another beautiful bank house in Madras.

My parents espoused a conservative branch of Protestantism known as the Open Plymouth Brethren, wherein my father became an Elder. This was a lay ministry and my father often performed special services for births (dedications), marriages (weddings) and deaths (funerals). He also performed adult baptisms and preached. He was in demand as a lay preacher, and I remember trips to Whitefield or to villages where he preached. He had a magic lantern, fueled by generators, and in a coconut frond-covered shack he retold bible stories with glass slides. (I wonder what happened to all those slides. I hope someone still uses them in a remote village somewhere. Maybe the stories of Sita and Ram have intermingled with those of Joseph and Mary after all these years.) My dad spoke Tamil, he studied it with a tutor, so he could preach in that language, although he often spoke with two or three translators in different languages such as Malayalam or Telugu.

One summer, when my mother was having a difficult time with her health, Dad sent us up to Ooty where we collected some good memories. We stayed at Montauban, a missionary retreat center that is still there. I climbed trees and played with the children in the compound.

My mother studied the Bible and became a devoted follower of Jesus Christ, which she is to this day. In the early 1940s, when I was a very young child, I witnessed her adult baptism in a small church in

Ooty which was at that time part of Montauban. Isabel receives her strength from the Bible and believes the promise:

> "They that wait upon the Lord shall renew their strength; they shall mount up with wings as eagles; they shall run, and not be weary; and they shall walk, and not faint."

> — ISAIAH 40:31 KJV

My mother developed her organizing skills and started charities to mitigate the obvious need around her. By the 1960s, she was getting parcels of used Christmas cards from America, which she remade for the Indian market and sold to fellow churchgoers and others, giving all the proceeds to her church charities. She organized picnics for the young people, set up a library and at one point had enough money from this effort to send a young Anglo-Indian to college. Her picnics were legendary.

Letters home to England from the Raj, written in tantalizing words, created the pictures of picnicking families sitting on tapestried rugs with their servants in the background hovering, ready to serve more tea. This may have happened, as some old photos attest, but not on our picnics.

Chamundi Hill, outside Mysore and not far from Bangalore, is a favorite spot for picnics and we often went there as a family or in a group. To get to the picnic place, a long bus ride was always required, unless we were a small enough group to go by car. Up the winding roads we would go, the sight of the Wodeyar maharajah's palaces diminishing as we drew near the top while that of the Chamundeeswari temples, the colossal Nandi bull (known as the mount of Shiva) and the vanquished demon with his huge sword and rigid snake expanded in size. Sometimes my mother's picnics would have a hundred young people going along with dekshi's of biryani in the back of a bus for lunch. My mother's wisdom was clear "the picnic begins on the bus". This turned out to be sage advice for all of life: instead of waiting for something to begin in the future, enjoy the ride.

At a picnic site near Colombo in Sri Lanka the coconut palms grew right up to the waves. Picnics were a heavily chaperoned event and one time, I got into trouble for taking an innocent walk away from the group with a heart-connection I had. My mother had some strong ideas as to where I should be and with whom. She tried to get me interested in Gavin who sadly died at thirty, but she vetoed Carl who she said took me to the "wrong" church and an Indian prince for having the "wrong" religion.

A picnic trip to Chamundi Hill with the Marretts in 1948

When I finished high school in Ooty, I lived at home for a year and a half taking stenography classes—typing and shorthand in Cochin. But then I got myself into college in Madras a quarter late. I was accepted on a minority seat because I was an Anglo-Indian. (I understand these seats have since been removed.)

After finishing college in Madras, I left India and came to the American Midwest on a scholarship to Bethel College in St. Paul,

Minnesota. I then attended graduate school at the University of Wisconsin and became a librarian. My mother sustained me during those lean years, although she could not send rupees or buy foreign exchange. She asked the ladies who had been sending her those used Christmas cards to send me dollars and warm clothing in exchange for hundreds of silk scarves she had had made from sari material, which they sold. I had some pocket money until I could get permission to work and a Green Card which meant I was a resident of the United States.

Me at an International event at the University of Wisconsin 1964.

It was over five years before I saw my mother again. By this time, my parents had immigrated to Australia, having given up (I recently learned) their right to immigrate to the United States to secure my passage. My sister Margo followed me, but she went to Canada and eventually to Australia. My younger sister Jen came to California and my brother, who originally went to Brisbane, Australia with our parents, now lives in Auckland, New Zealand. We created our own family diaspora. My mother, who was born and grew up in India, never had an Indian passport because she was able to obtain a British passport after Independence as her father was born in England. When she came to Australia in 1968, she applied for an Australian passport and got one within a year. However, that little road in Bangalore that was named for her great great-grandfather is still called Clapham Street in Richmond Town.

My parents tithed their income from early in their marriage, whatever hardships it created. My father gave thanks when he discovered, and shared with my mother, that since the day they had started tithing ten years earlier, his income had increased ten times. They believed that this was the blessing of the Lord. It was with her faith that my mother also prospered in her businesses. My dad, in his retirement, would stroke her right hand and call it the "money hand." This probably comes from Tamilian folklore, which puts an emphasis on the importance of our hands. "Kai varamate" meant that a person was not generous, implying a person's hand simply did not come forward to give. Food must be mixed by hand when cooking to sweeten it. Sometimes a prayer "bless the hands that cooked this meal" is offered. Being Anglo-Indian means we have rich roots in both India and Britain, Tamil, and English.

Dad's pension, however large and important it had been in India, was now reduced by the dollar-rupee exchange in Australia. My mother took in students to make ends meet. She got a job in a café waiting tables. She told me of one occasion when she felt mortified when a former acquaintance walked in and exclaimed, "Mrs. Chase, bank manager's wife, waiting tables!" My parents believed that there was no shame in honest work. She started her own business, selling lace products from Narsipur in Andhra State—doilies, cushion covers, duchesse sets, tablecloths—all made with mercerized cotton thread on steel crochet hooks in old Irish patterns learned from Irish missionaries. Those crochet needles were made from bicycle spokes.

With my dad sometimes accompanying her as the driver in Brisbane, Australia, my mother, Isabel, would take a suitcase of lace to a home where she sold it on the party plan, like Tupperware. Soon, there were more parties than she could handle, and she commissioned other sellers. Isabel quit her day job. She hand-wrote all the receipts and kept the accounts on pieces of paper or scribbled them in a book. My dad became the accountant, but I remember him telling me that he would go over all her accounts before banking the money and they were never a penny off. This was a trait she had probably honed when she had a big household to maintain and several staff to manage—mali (gardener), cook, sweeper, head of staff, day and night watchmen, a dhobi (washer man) and, when the children were little, an ayah (nanny)—some of whom were supplied by the bank because of Dad's position. The cook spent part of an hour each day recounting his expenditures in the market—fresh coconuts, coriander, mutton, tamarind, snake kai and okra— every anna accounted for to my Mum.

My parents, Stephen, and Isabel Chase, shortly after they emigrated to Australia.

Isabel was an unrelentingly stern disciplinarian, particularly with me, the eldest. If I got 99/100 for a test, she demanded to know what happened to that 1 point. I had to memorize long poems, like The Master's Hand: "It was battered and scarred/and the auctioneer thought/it hardly worth his while..." for nine long verses. But Isabel could be incredibly generous as well. I remember attending a wedding once when the bride's mother admonished her for buying a dish as a gift. Surprised, I pressed my mother, "Why didn't she want you to buy a present?" I asked. She finally relented and told me it was because she had paid for the whole wedding for this Anglo-Indian family because they could not afford it. Other times, when we owned a cow, she would take the extra milk to church and give it away. She would make me Gulab jamuns by the dozens and send them to my boarding school so that I could share them with my friends. She did not want me to have to hide in the bathroom and eat my sweets alone, like one of the other girls did.

Lace products from Andhra that my mother, Isabel sold in Australia.

My parents bought land outside of Bangalore in Whitefield as an investment. This area was considered a good place to settle all the

Anglo-Indians in India, an impossible task. Anglo-Indians were a problem politically because they were mis-read to have dual loyalties. Some thought they could solve this by giving us barren land to till and letting us create our own school system. Little did they realize that we would emigrate to all the English-speaking countries of the world and our schools would be the most sought after in India. My parents decided to donate the six acres in Whitefield to the Steward's Association in trust for the indigenous Christian work in India. It has proven a good investment (for this charity) because it is worth lakhs of rupees now thanks to the burgeoning technology industry there. A lakh is 1,00,000 and a crore is worth ten million or a hundred lakhs in the Indian Numbering System.

With my mother's lace business doing well in Australia, Isabel and Stephen bought a house in the suburb of Auchenflower in Brisbane. They bought other houses, an apartment complex, a small office building, and they also built a 3-story office building where my mother had her business on the upstairs floor for many years. That was after she moved it out of the basement of her Queensland home, where they had built out the area below the house that was originally built on stilts. They used the basement of the office building as a warehouse and rented the main floor to a baker. My dad said that it was a charitable business to give away free bread to the Australians because it continuously lost money. Eventually, they sold the bakery, and it became Brumby's, a successful Australian bread chain (not ours).

The lace business prospered. My mother had a hundred saleswomen selling lace all over Australia. When my sister, Margo's first husband died in Toronto, Canada she sought Australian immigration for herself and her young son, Timmy. The way I remember the story is that she was a teacher and the Australian government thought they had enough teachers, but when she told them she would be working for our mother, who employed several Australians, then she had no problems. When my mother was seventy and decided to retire, my sister Margo bought the lace business and ran it for another twenty years.

My mother at 95 with her children: Jennifer, Eric, mum, myself, and Margo. 2016

Generations of women in our family have stories that sustain us. One is that only the strong came to India and followed their husbands into the jungle, if need be. This was the stock we came from. Nothing was an obstacle to optimistic survival. This is an Anglo-Indian credo. My father died in 1993 and my mother took up his gardening and stayed on in their large five-bedroom house until her eighties. She sold all her properties and banked the money in certificates of deposit, generously giving her adult children gifts and losing nothing during the economic downturn. My mother turned 100 on February 7, 2021, and she still supports many indigenous missionaries in India. After the tsunami, she raised enough money to build a new church in Port Blair in the Andamans. She is very involved in life, until recently cooking up a storm of our favorite Anglo-Indian dishes whenever we visited her —vermicelli pilau, beef tongue made by putting two tongues in a circle and weighting it down with a stone until it became deli meat, pork vindaloo, meat ball curry, cabbage foogarth, or carrot halvah. Her grandchildren favored her pepper water. My sister has taken on the task of making Gulab Jamuns and many other favorites. My mother still enjoys a baked custard that my sister now bakes, but I miss the custards she used to make for me.

Isabel loves to play *Scrabble* online. She is an expert after playing Scrabble with my dad every week since 1956 when it was first distributed internationally. As always, my mother, Isabel, is the quintessential Anglo-Indian woman. You can try to beat her at Scrabble if you want. Good luck!

Isabel admiring a lace tablecloth for sale.

When I was traveling in India once my mother wrote to me: "I got into bed at nine-thirty and woke up a few minutes before midnight, so I thanked the Lord for all that had passed and trust Him for all that is to come and then I went back to sleep again." Isabel has received her letter from the Queen to commemorate her one-hundredth birthday! We celebrated with an international family zoom, which was all we could do during the Covid-19 pandemic. I have gratitude for my mother and for her inspiring life. None of the things she taught me have gone to waste.

Published originally in *The Local News Magazine* in the Nilgiris as Ninety Plus. Publisher and Editor: Edwin David. The Local Media Publishing Co. December 5, 2011.

9

CHURCHES AND MISSIONARIES

Europeans had their heads filled with Greek, Roman or Celtic myths, even though the Church had suppressed all overt worship of Minerva, Zeus, Diana or Pan in the first century. Nevertheless, with a Eurocentric catholic aversion, they were put off by the Hindu pantheon which included Saraswathi, Lakshmi, Sita, Ram and Krishna. With the blessing of the government of England, hordes of missionaries swarmed into India to convert the indigenous Hindu, Muslim, or Buddhist to Christianity. The effect on Hinduism was minimal, as followers believe in one Great Soul or Athma. Hinduism embraces all forms of worship, so Christianity was simply incorporated into its fold without abandoning its core. Since Anglo-Indians were westernized in their customs, they followed the basic tenants of Christianity. They were Roman Catholic, Baptist, Methodist, Pentecostals, and Plymouth Brethren. After Independence, Christians in India brought together the various formal protestant denominations to create the Church of South India and the Church of North India. The Wesleyan Methodist Church became a part of the Church of South India, although it had an all-Hindu choir in Madras. Similarly, the Church of North India is an amalgamation of four protestant denominations.

The Raj Era was a time of missionaries. Although many held the belief that all must hear the message of Christ and had a sincere desire to bring Christianity to India, there were also others who became missionaries to escape—whether from their own unsatisfactory lives (sometimes disinherited as the younger sons), the Irish famines, or the damp, cold, dark winters of England's climes.

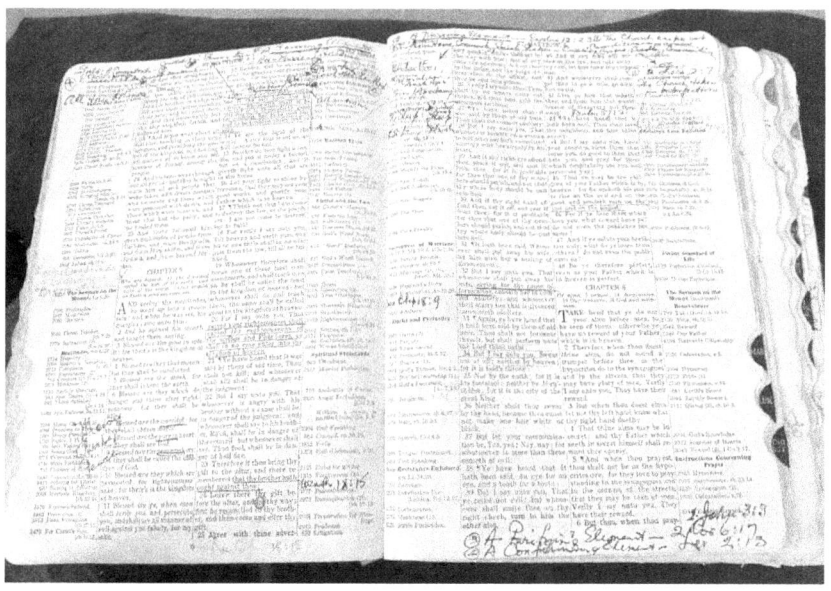

Pages from my dad's marked up bible which he had most of his adult life

William Carey (1761-1834), the founder of the Baptist Missionary Society, was larger than life. He was a missionary in India from 1792 to the end of his life. His immense body of work involved many translations of the Bible into Indian languages, as well as many Indian language dictionaries, grammar texts and botanical texts. Even now, over 200 years later, the Baptist Missionary Society's World Mission, carries on his vision in many parts of the globe. During Carey's early work in Bengal, he once had to seek refuge in the Danish colony of Serampore because of the East India Company's oppressive authority and a policy forbidding proselytizing of indigenous Indian peoples. This was a policy that they later abandoned but India now bans Christian missionaries. In a role reversal, there are currently many Hindu and Buddhist "missionaries" in the West.

At the very beginning of the Christian era in India, long before William Carey's new wave of converts were baptized in India's rivers and water storage tanks, St. Thomas himself is said to have come to India and preached. Driving past the ancient Kapaleeswara temple in Mylapore to St. Thomas' Mount, you will find a great church in Madras. Under this church is a cave with the preserved and enshrined footprints of the disciple Thomas. Thousands of children have visited this site on field trips, climbed the hundred and thirty-four steps and seen the artifacts.

My father told me stories that he was told as a boy of large massacres of Christians in the areas around St. Thomas' Mount centuries before. The Portuguese established the shrine there around 1520, which may have led to later retaliation. British missionaries followed, and eventually a colony of Anglo-Indians settled around St. Thomas' Mount. Some still live there.

In Old Goa there is established a UNESCO World Heritage site because of its many large churches—some as big as those in Rome. St. Francis Xavier came to Old Goa as a missionary, where the relic of his body is housed in a shrine. Many of these beautiful churches are being restored, but sometimes the ruins are just as interesting, having been damaged in political and religious skirmishes hundreds of years ago.

There is an ancient Christian sect called the Syrian Christians in Kerala. They still sing their hymns in Syriac, and they believe that their religion is as old as Christianity itself. Christianity has a stronger hold in Kerala than any other state—as Syrians, Jacobites, Marthomites, Catholics and Pentecostals. Each year a revival is held in the sandy riverbed of the Pamba River in Kerala. It is called the Maramon Christian Convention and it attracts over fifty thousand people. I attended this convention with my father when he spoke with several translators. At that time, I could still code in shorthand, and I remember taking notes furiously, but they are all lost. The Maramon Convention is enormous and keeps on going.

From the days of William Carey to the time of Independence, missionaries from many countries came to India. I attended a missionary school in the Nilgiri Hills of south India, Breeks Memorial, which my mother attended a generation before me. This was not a school where missionaries taught the villagers to read and write or took care of orphans and translated the bible, but a school for the children of the missionaries.

A Canadian missionary, Catherine Munro, had adopted my friend, Wendy Mongol. Wendy's father was the head of her tribe of Sora people in Assam. When her mother died at her birth, her father brought her as an infant to be taken care of by Miss Munro. Miss Munro took care of many children, but she considered Wendy her own first born and brought her back to Canada when she retired. Indira Gandhi was a good friend of Miss Catherine Munro. Whenever Miss Munro went to Delhi, she would pay a visit to her friend, Indira. They had a mutual admiration. As a young woman in Canada, Miss Munro felt the call to go to India, but her betrothed felt called to go to Africa. She parted from him and lived in India by herself for forty years. Most of the people in Orissa are Oriya but there are many tribes. Miss Munro worked with the Sora tribe, translating the Bible into Sora and helping to improve the lot of the Sora people, including adopting several other children. She was much revered and loved by them.

My friend Anne still spoke fluent Hindi although she later studied Hebrew and Vietnamese. Her parents, the Buffams, were missionaries in the Bombay area. There were other missionaries: The Ponds, Pospisals, Goulds, Neeches, Pritchards, McDonalds (Salvation Army), the Andersons, the Durhams and many other families we knew. Dr. Neech delivered so many babies a week in India that when she went back to England and tried to get a job, they could not believe her record. My friend Eunice, whose parents were missionaries in north India, told a story of horror about the time she and her brothers were put off a train during the murderous times of the partition of India. Another friend, whose parents were missionaries in China, tells of how they and her siblings walked out of a village to leave China at the time of the cultural revolution and their guides were killed upon returning. Being a missionary was an arduous and sacrificial calling.

Breeks Memorial School in Ooty (from the back facing the fountain)

These missionaries were "laboring in the field" most of the year, but during the hot summers they went up to the hills to recuperate. My father, who worked full time year-round at the bank, would go out on weekends to preach to the old ladies and small families who needed the blessing of their churches when the missionaries left. He did not take the summers off.

Some thoughtful missionaries kept their children in India, in boarding schools, to avoid long separations. Many missionary children (MKs are Missionary Kids) did not appreciate being sent away at all and felt the family separation intensely. Some of them suffered post-traumatic stress syndrome (PTSD) and needed years of therapy after these intense separations.

One missionary woman who sent her children to school in England for many years, told how she got on a bus to go to the home where her son was living. She didn't realize until she got there that the good-looking young man who got off the bus with her was her son. Neither recognized the other.

The evangelism of missionaries existed on many levels, from the high Church of England with its rituals, sacraments, and priests to the low churched Brethren with relatively little emphasis on the liturgy.

My father and his friends sometimes preached on a street corner. He sang hymns and choruses while he played his guitar and young people and kids distributed tracts to passersby, usually in an Anglo-Indian neighborhood. I liked the tambourines especially. Sometimes my father was invited to preach in a small town or village although he also preached in the big cities of Madras, Bangalore and Calcutta.

Anglo-Indians were Christians, but sometimes held onto old superstitions. Once, when my dad was very ill and, in the hospital, he heard that a mongoose had fallen off our roof and died, and he was cheered no end. He told me that it was an old Tamil myth that when someone was dying in a house an animal may give its life instead. Although he claimed he was not superstitious, the old ways died hard. One day, years later, I was ill one night. The next morning when I found a dead rat in my pool, I remembered this story and felt better already.

Christians are a small minority in India today, whether Anglo-Indian or indigenous. Christmas is no longer a holiday in India. There are so many religions and so many New Year's Days that Indians are allowed to take thirteen holy days each year, whichever they deem sacred. The shops, however, celebrate everyone's holy days, hoping to make an extra rupee for each one. You can still see lighted stars at Christmas, carefully crafted from thin bamboo strips and tissue paper, and hoisted high up over Christian homes.

Our family had a white star that was four feet across. Although we never had a 'real' Christmas tree in tropical India, we had a close facsimile acquired by robbing a large branch from a Casuarina tree farm or plantation on the edge of town. Casuarina is grown in India for firewood. We would drive out for miles to find the perfect branch to decorate with handmade paper chains and lights. Stealing a branch off one of these large trees was an Anglo-Indian tradition. It wasn't as if we could just drive around the block and find a lot filled with fir trees in India.

*Mrs. Tiessen, Mrs. Buffam and Mrs. Gould, missionaries in India whose children
(pictured) David and Ann Buffam and Florence Gould went to Breeks with me.
Taken in the late 1950s (Photo: Shari Buffam Donaldson)*

PART TWO
ECHOES AND CONFLICTS

10

ANGLO-INDIANS AND THE RAJ LIFE

T ales of the good life in India sprang up and traveled with the gypsies and caravans crossing the continents of Asia and Europe, and with the merchants from China to Arabia as they traveled the Silk Road. From those tales, mysterious and beguiling pictures of a magical land began to form in the minds of eager listeners all over the world. It was these stories that first attracted the British to India. Colonization, profitability, societal stratification, and proselytization came later.

In the tradition of immigrants and travelers everywhere, stories sent home to England were always of "the good life"—sometimes true, often imagined, exaggerated or incomplete. Stories of a beautiful life were shared by the writers and storytellers of the time. Caparisoned elephants, precision camel battalions, military horses going back to the time of Alexander the Great (and before), rajahs and maharajas (minor and major kings) with their ranis (queens) and begums (wives) with retinues of servants were all part of the lore.

British-Indian life, later known as the Raj Era, sparked the imaginations of many with memories and snippets of letters glorifying the era. (The Raj Period is more precisely recorded as those years when Britain had direct rule over the Indian subcontinent from 1858 to

1947 and, Anglo-Indian history goes back to the first European forays about 500 years ago.) But, when Warren Hastings, the first Governor General of India, read his defense during his famous seven-year impeachment trial, he painted a picture of India with mountains of gold on each side tempting him to corruption and self-aggrandizement. One vicereine came to India with her French maid and housekeeping staff and proceeded to hire a dozen Indian employees to complete her care. Even Englishmen and women of lower ranks were able to employ some household help. Englishmen who married Portuguese Luso-Indians or other Indian women (Hindu or Muslim) created the verifiable Anglo-Indians, those of mixed heritage who were born in India and lived a life during the Raj that belongs to a time gone by—an era now left to the imagination and a way of life that that bridged the east and the west.

Although the Raj Era ended almost seventy-five years ago, many expatriates from that Raj life would try to recreate it today if they could find a way. Not the political realities of ruler and ruled, subject and lord, but the subtle nuances of the good life that the Raj symbolized to them then and that endures in the minds of those now in the diaspora, both British and Anglo-Indian, and in the minds of their children and grandchildren, many of whom know nothing of India itself.

LIVING THE GOOD LIFE

In the minds of those who lived during the Raj, the storied elegance of this period epitomized the good life. Despite its distance in geography and time, this fantastical, faraway, seemingly exotic life can be woven into our present day lives, if only by using an antique peacock fan, a deeply colored and embroidered silk drape or a pashmina shawl. The Raj life does not have to be left in the shadows of browning pages in libraries. "The good life haunts us," wrote Yi-Fu Tuan, Emeritus Professor of Geography at the University of Wisconsin in his book, *The Good Life*. Living the good life is a habit and a choice that includes fantasy and reflection, austerity, and discipline. There are always whiners, detractors, rewriters of history and revisionists; but it is the essence that counts. The essence of the Raj life can be recreated with simple accouterments—a whitewashed wall; a tablecloth of smooth, crocheted, ecru cotton lace; a sandalwood box; and the aroma of a curry cooking on the stove with cardamom, cinnamon, and curry leaves enhancing its flavors. It lives on in the attitudes of the people, caring for each other through many misfortunes and surviving in India or abroad.

It is a challenge to identify your own concept of the good life, and then to create that life within the context of your own space and time. We can choose to live the Raj life, recreating the fantasy of a bygone era by means of the delicious tastes and smells, the artifacts and experiences that grounded it and made it earthy and alive. Disembarking, as it were, from the pages of a nineteenth-century novel of the Raj, you might light a mildly incense-scented candle in a mango-shaped stand and drink the heady perfume of the past, without the negative side effects of cholera and death.

When Anglo-Indians left India after Independence in 1947, they took with them a cooking tradition of full-bodied aromatic curries, flavorful soups and transporting meat dishes. A rich mixture of an English diet intertwined with Indian spices and sauces; their foods were cooked in a particular way associated only with this community in India. They borrowed freely from both Indian and British recipes to create a cuisine they called their own.

The most intriguing aroma coming from the royal kitchen was curry. It is said that Queen Victoria insisted that curry be on her lunch menu every day. It was served with great ceremony by two resplendently dressed Indians in her retinue. As Empress of India at the peak of British colonization, she could say that the sun never set on the British Empire. It meant that wherever one wandered on earth there was a Union Jack flying in that time zone. India left its mark on British society, just as Britain left its stamp on India.

THE BRITISH STAMP

The influence of Britain on India, the source of the phrase "The Raj Life," lasted three centuries, although the Raj royal aspect, which covered India, Pakistan, Bangladesh, Burma, and Singapore, began in 1858 when Queen Victoria took over from the East India Company as Empress. It ended in 1947 when India gained its independence and George VI was king. This short period of almost ninety years was augmented by those earlier years when the British traded with India via the East India Company (EIC), which was established in 1600. The EIC (initially known as the John Company), virtually ruled India with its own armies and regulations, until it was dissolved in deference to the crown in 1858. Britain's influence on India was both lasting and pervasive. India's influence on Britain was equally tenacious.

During the British Raj era in India, on a sliding calendar from ninety to three hundred years—1600 to 1947 and a few years beyond —the Raj life was not as glorious as it aspired to be. There was pestilence and disease— cholera, Kala Azar (black fever), tuberculosis, smallpox, plague and typhoid. Childbirth in the unsterile conditions of the times was hazardous. Birth control was as efficient as self-control, and families of ten children were not uncommon. Many women married three and even four times just to survive, and men married just as often to ensure their own survival after the deaths of their spouses. Divorce was almost impossible to get, and so it was both unknown and ostracized. Scandal was rampant, but legal divorces were rare. Through it all, the persistent dream of the Raj life is ensconced, deeply held as the gold standard of an ideal lifestyle, however rare its true existence. The Raj life was equivalent to The Good Life in the minds of Indo-Britains, and of those who read about it, heard the stories, or felt the smooth softness of a Mysore silk, tasted the bittersweet, flavorful leaves of Assam or Nilgiris tea and inhaled the deep perfume of jasmine

The Raj life, in the end, has nothing to do with feeling superior (as the British often did) or being treated as inferior (as Indians and Anglo-Indians often were). Colonization is, in and of itself, untenable. In the new millennium you don't have to worry about what color your skin will turn if you step out of the shade, or how many servants you have, or who's been to whose house for tea—or political or economic geographies. You are free to enjoy the past, as you imagine it, the best of both worlds—Indian and British—The Good Life. As Nobel Prize-winning writer, Rabindranath Tagore advocated, "We have to find some basis that is universal, that is eternal, and we have to discover those things which have an everlasting value. We had to build our own world with our own thoughts and energy of mind." —*The Essential Tagore*. Or, as my mother, Isabel, might say: "Try to forget the sad and the bad while you remember the good and savor the best." That could be the essence of the Raj life to Anglo-Indians.

Samuel Clemens, who used the pseudonym Mark Twain, described India in his 1896 book *Following the Equator: A Journey Around the World:*

"This is indeed India! The land of dreams and romance, of fabulous wealth and fabulous poverty, of splendor and rags, of palaces and hovels, of famine and pestilence, of genii and giants and Aladdin lamps, of tigers and elephants, the cobra and the jungle, the country of a hundred nations and a hundred tongues, of a thousand religions and two million gods, cradle of the human race, birthplace of human speech, mother of history, grandmother of legend, great-grandmother of traditions, whose yesterday's bear date with the moldering antiquities for the rest of nations-the one sole country under the sun that is endowed with an imperishable interest for alien prince and alien peasant, for lettered and ignorant, wise and fool, rich and poor, bond and free, the one land that all men desire to see, and having seen once, by even a glimpse, would not give that glimpse for the shows of all the rest of the world combined."

11

THE ANGLO-INDIANS

When I tell people I'm Anglo-Indian, the question they most often ask, is: "Which half?" I am very tempted to reply: "the top half" or "my right side." What do they mean? Think about Mendel's Law—tall beans, broad beans, and string beans are randomly assigned genetically. Why would humans be different? I wonder if some people really think that your genes stay unmixed somewhere in your body or your brain. I explain that there was not just one brave English soldier and one Rajput princess, but thousands of British soldiers and thousands of Indian or Eurasian women who married and had child-bearing liaisons from the 1600s to the 1900s. Even though laws of exclusion were at times enforced on Anglo-Indians, "mixed marriages" continued, as they do to this day all over the world. Thousands of children of such mixed couples in India became a distinct community, the Anglo-Indian community, with its own traditions, history, and stories.

Stringent laws were enacted against intermarriage after 1857. The publication of Charles Darwin's book, *On the Origin of Species by Means of Natural Selection: The Preservation of Favored Races in the Struggle for Life in 1859* also influenced these laws against mingling of the privileged and underprivileged races. Anglo-Indians married each other as a result. Occasionally, an Englishman would marry a domiciled woman, as my grandfather Harry Shepherd did when he came from Norfolk to India and married my grandmother, Florence Lilywhite. Her family whose maternal line goes way back in India.

My grandparents: my grandmother married on the trust stating that she was British as attested by his commanding officer.

The name was sometimes spelled with one el and sometimes with two, Lilywhite or Lillywhite. My mother always spelled her name with one el (as do I) but when she met her Bombay cousins years later, she found they spelled the name with two els. Patrick Lilywhite (my great-grandfather) used various spellings in his many locations.

How do we know, for sure, that there was never a "Rajput princess" in someone's past, or a Luso-Indian (who was mixed-Portuguese)? The names on my family tree are English, but we have family legends. One prevailing story is that a (British) Chase ancestor married an Indian woman and the child, Stephen, turned out to be light skinned. In the racist and legally prejudicial past, light skin meant you could "pass" for English. The English Chase ancestor was Richard Chase, who was born in 1762. Richard wanted to take his son Stephen with him back to England, leaving his Indian wife (the child's mother) behind. The mother took her son, Stephen, to a temple and had a long caste mark tattooed on his forehead, making him unsuitable for English society. Stephen and the generations that followed stayed in India until my father (also named Stephen Chase) immigrated to Australia in 1967. I wish I had more information about the Stephen with the cast mark who, I was told, became a preacher in Madras. One time, my father took me to the old church now a Tamil language church near the Adyar River in Madras where the Stephen Chase of our history used to preach. It was just on the other side of the river from the old Connemara Hotel.

My dad's diary of dates for October 1958-May 1967

My dad taught us that we had inherited the British imagination and the Indian mental capacity—the British preference for order, precision, and planning and the Indian ability to accept chaos, work through any obstruction and persevere. Although come to think of it, Indians are extremely detailed, too. If blue British blood runs in our veins, then India runs in our red-blooded arteries. Britain was our fatherland, but India was and will always be our motherland. I am a grandchild of the Raj, but, even more so, I am a great great-grandchild of India.

We have passports—that allows us to live and work in a specific place, and sometimes our sons and daughters fight that country's wars or represent them in sports especially cricket or hockey. The choice of domicile is economic and political. As Yogi Vishwamji Maharaj said on his arrival in America;

> "I don't have any strange feelings. The countries of this world are like rooms of a house. I have come from one room into another. But if you ask me how I feel about my house, this world, I'd say I feel very happy!"

This is exactly the philosophy embraced by most Anglo-Indians. A passport or citizenship is merely a piece of paper, a means of passage and residence; it does not represent a feeling of the heart. We are loyal to our countries of domicile and our children travel all over the earth. We have gone to bat, quite literally, under every flag, but it is India we hold dear and from whence grow our roots. India is the central room of our house.

Australia and Canada had "White Policies" for immigration until the 1960s. America's "white policy" was based on a quota set by a census of the white population in the United States in the 1800s, but this has changed. When I visited New Zealand in 1968, I was given a questionnaire asking if I was European, Polynesian, or Indian, based on their local ethnicities. Now they call New Zealand "Aotearoa," (its Maori name), and welcome immigrants. Anglo-Indians have migrated to all countries. As the cliché goes: "You can take the Anglo-Indian out of India, but you can never take India out of the Anglo-Indian."

Sometimes the British who came to India from England would go back for a season or two, then take the next chance they got to return to India. Who wanted to sit in a chilly drawing room, watching those drizzly rain drops on the windowpanes when one could be in India, where it truly rained, monsoons and typhoons, and where the sun shone brighter than bright? India was where the good food was—curry and rice instead of stew. Today you can get Chicken Tikka in every city in England because of our Indian influence.

In India, when the sun set, it did not linger. Twilight was over almost before it began. Fireflies came out, too numerous to count, darting this way and that, lighting up the cool evening in a way that no lighted cigarette could. Likewise, dawn had better catch you waiting when it made its quick curtsey before the day began.

Those who came to the colonies as wives or ladies, but who never allowed India into their bosoms, lost out. It was as if life passed them by, busy as they were with durbars and receptions of state. Fear gripped them, and they wrote their fear-filled tales and sent them home, while the more adventurous women lived on in India. These were the Anglo-Indian women whose parasols shot up as they walked sprightly and sandal-footed through the marketplace, choosing mangoes, guavas, papayas, and tender green coconuts for their helpers to carry, happily bargaining for tight white jasmine buds. To them, India was no mystery, no hidden path. They cooked the curries and sautéed the meat, boiled the rice, or made parathas and developed a cuisine that blended Portuguese with Maharashtrian, British with Telugu and Tamilian. Their inventiveness and culinary excitement were passed on to the next generations. Dry curry mixed breadcrumbs with a hot sauce; glacé was French with a nice bite to it; stuffed squash turned into stuffed snake coys with ground beef curry; and an Irish stew was livened up with green chilies.

These women spoke several languages. My grandmother spoke Hindustani fluently, and could even curse in it. My great-grandmother could speak Tamil as well. The real Anglo-Indians translated and transcribed for the British who were Anglo-Indian only for a season. Early in the history of Britain in India, the English who had not intermarried were also called Anglo-Indians. "Mixed-blood" Anglo-Indians were the conduits that channeled the Raj. They managed the railroads and kept the telegraphs running. They ran the customs department, day and night. The trains were always on time with their Anglo-Indian drivers. They taught in English-medium schools all over the country.

THE EARLY YEARS

By the late eighteenth century, Anglo-Indians, being of mixed ancestry, were excluded from the mainstream British Army. Anglo-Indians, as such, were not clearly defined at that time and the rule covered anyone who was born in India, known as "country born." Perhaps this was the true origin of the recipe "Country Captain." It took a hundred years to sort out who were British, wherever they were born, and who was "mixed" (if it ever was sorted out). Author Rumer Godden was born in Sussex but went to India before she was a year old and spent most of her life there. John Masters, who cast aspersions on country-born Anglo-Indians and railway colonies in his novel, Bhowani Junction, was the grandson of William Masters, headmaster of a school in Calcutta from 1836-1844. The Mountbattens, Earl Mountbatten of Burma and Edwina, were tied to India in many ways. Edwina was from South Africa, of Dutch and French background, and they were married in New Delhi. Earl Mountbatten's father accompanied Edward VII, then Prince of Wales, to India in 1875, and his brother King George V in 1911. Earl Mountbatten was the last Viceroy and the first Governor-General of independent India.

Many Anglo-Indians also called England 'home' although that was a bit of a delusion. My friend's mother who we only called Mrs. Rahman was really English born in England and married to an Indian she had met in London. All the years she was in India she talked about going 'home' to England one day; but when her son emigrated and brought her to stay with him in England, she could think of nothing but going back 'home' to India. It only took one cold winter for her to say, "Son, I want to go back home." Soon she did return, and she played gin rummy at her Club until she died happy in her old age. Home is where your heart is. India is in our hearts.

India is a place that writes itself into your soul. It is not to be trifled with. When you encounter India on a soul level, it will never recede into the background of your life even if you try to push it away. Memories only become more vivid and a longing to return grows more intense. Many who want to go back to India cannot, for many reasons, and they die with their desire unfulfilled. As Anita Nair has written, I "understand why the British were so reluctant to leave India and return to the bleak white cliffs of Dover." India will never become a distant memory but will always feel like something that happened just yesterday. The tastes, the sounds, the moving video of people and foods involving all our senses, even the dust, the grit, the indelible dirt is seared into our minds and viscerally in our bodies.

In the eighteenth century, life outside the barracks was much nicer than inside. Any married man was able to collect some extra rupees (or pagodas) for his family as an allowance. There was a rumor among later-arriving English women that those earlier marriages to Indians were immoral and illegal, but this was not accurate. For the most part, Englishmen did enter into marriage with local women and the India Office kept records of these unions covering over a century. There were also alliances and dalliances, fueled by the seductive aroma of spices to be sure. These became solidified over the generations when the children of these relationships entered into matrimony with other such children. *The Jewel in the Crown* or *Staying On*, by Paul Scott, does not do justice to the gross numbers of Europeans in India. In the mid-1800s there were over 200,000 Anglo-Indians in the British security forces alone, and that did not include the civilians who were planters and traders or working in administration.

At one point, Anglo-Indians were relegated to be drummers and fifers. Fifers were non-combatant foot soldiers who accompanied bands and gave signals for formation changes. Anglo-Indians also occupied some of the medical branches as apothecaries and physicians.

ANGLO-INDIAN CULTURE AND SOCIETY

Most Anglo-Indians never knew, never met, and never even saw the lords and ladies who have been much written about. We didn't know the Edens, the Clives, the Hastings or the Cannings. Lady Stow invited my parents over for tea, in the early 1940s, to thank my dad for taking care of her business so well at the bank. When Queen Elizabeth visited India in 1960 my parents were invited to a reception for her in Bangalore. We, the Anglo-Indians, were a part of the Raj and we lived it every day, but only in the most ordinary of ways. We brought the Raj and India together by being in the middle, as it were.

There were some attempts to gather up all the Anglo-Indians in India and send them out to the typhoid-ridden, convict-occupied Andaman Islands. Another idea was to build a town for them to be separate from the rest of India, but together and independent. Whitefield (near Bangalore) was one such community, built in concentric circles with a Church of England in one slice of the pie. Lately, it has become known as the place of Sai Baba; but during the Raj it was a community of mostly British and Anglo-Indians. Around 1892 His Highness, Chamaraja Wodeyar, the Maharaja of Mysore, granted 3900 acres of land to the Eurasian and Anglo-Indian Association (E&AI) of Mysore and Coorg, to establish agricultural settlements at Whitefield. Inadequate sanitation and lack of proper schools made life difficult, and after 1947 most of the population left. There was not much means of making a living out in Whitefield then, and Anglo-Indians, although not above growing a few chili bushes, were not agriculturalists. In the early 1900s there was nothing like the recent establishment of the Bangalore tech farms in the Whitefield area.

At the beginning of the Raj, Anglo-Indians and Britons were restricted from owning land in India. Anglo-Indians overcame this restriction after being ostracized by the British, particularly after the war of 1857. Perhaps if they had been farming people, their history would have been very different. McCluskieganj (in Bihar) was founded through the enterprise of Timothy McCluskie as an independent homeland and nation for Anglo-Indians and was home to 400 Anglo-Indian families. They grew flowers and vegetables for sale, but again, after 1947, most of the population left. Over 100,000 Anglo-Indians emigrated from the time of India's Independence through the early 1950s. My mother insists that Anglo-Indians knew that England would be cold, and it was especially when living through the post-War years, but they still felt they could endure and give their children a better life where they could compete and rise.

SOCIAL ORGANIZATIONS

Anglo-Indians and the British had their own organizations, social clubs, and sports teams, many of them still exist today. The Tollygunj Club in Calcutta had a varied history over 300 years. The Gymkhana Clubs held onto their British exclusivity until the end of the Raj. The East Indian Club of Calcutta currently has a new life in Melbourne, Australia. Some Anglo-Indians started their private clubs, such as The Bangalore Club and the Bowring Institute. The Rangers Club in Calcutta is over a hundred years old. There was a historical tension between Anglo-Indians of means and those of lesser means. For example, the Anglo-Indians in the Indian Medical Department (apothecaries and doctors) considered themselves above the members of the Railway Institute which meant they often belonged to different clubs and socialized separately.

Anglo-Indians, although intelligent and astute, love to eat, to dance and to gossip. The day after a dance, over kormas and dal, they would talk about who was at the dance, what they wore, with whom they danced and what they said. All of this was discussed in front of the staff, who then told their neighbors' staff, who told their madams, the memsahibs and the missys (young girls). This was possibly how we got to be such a close-knit community. Unless it was the tea—that daily afternoon pleasure of tea with all its accoutrements: curry puffs, freshly made peanut butter, guava jelly, lemon tarts, Madeira cake, mango fools, halvahs and strong tea with milk and cardamom, sometimes called chai or simply masala tea. The Raj was not just about dominance and European supremacy. Among Anglo-Indians, it was a pure example of embracing diversity.

The rain and damp of England, with an occasional peep hole of sunshine, could not compete with the direct rays of warmth in India. A shower of rain was not like a monsoon deluge, when it rained hard for three or four days in a row enlivening the earth to grow coconuts and sprout grains—rice, ragi, sago, tapioca and corn. Hurricanes came once or twice a year with their orgasmic blast of winds and storming gales that tossed the ocean like it was shaking a cocktail. The passion of a hurricane filled one with awe, even just watching from a window or balcony. Feeling the warm, hard drops on your skin, soaking through clothes to your bones in a minute, flashing thunderbolts and lightening so loud it bedazzled your eyes and pounded your ears. Trees fell or were uprooted, lakes swelled, and debris blew about. The catamaran beach dwellers were overwhelmed once again and those who chose to live in the riverbeds were forced to hurry away with their meagre belongings. Palm fronds flew past houses. Carpets literally took to the air, as if by magic. Daily activities stopped, you could not just sit and sip tea or read a book while Mother Nature was acting out so spectacularly. A hurricane, like a typhoon, demanded your full attention. The monsoons in the tropics left no room in your head for sad or sorry thoughts. Soon, the sun would return to shine down strong and dry everything up very quickly. The sun shines for over two hundred days a year in India.

The French, the Dutch, the Portuguese, and the Danes brought their ethnic histories to blend with the Indian to create a unique new people that still enjoy their culture and their diversity today. According to the *Constitution of India* Part XIX section 366 (2) an Anglo-Indian is defined as "a person whose father or any of whose other male progenitors in the male line is or was of European descent but who is domiciled within the territory of India and is or was born within such territory of parents habitually resident therein and not established there for temporary purposes only." https://www.india.gov.in/sites/upload_files/npi/files/coi_part_full.pdf

TRANQUEBAR

I can see it now: King Claudius in Shakespeare's *Hamlet* saying (in Tamil) from the ramparts of the newly restored Danish fort in a south Indian town: "Stay; give me chai Hamlet, this pearl is thine; Here's to thy health." Trumpets sound, and a cannon is shot.

The Danish East India Company was established in 1616, and soon the first fleet was sent out under command of the young nobleman, Ove Giedde. A Danish settlement called Tranquebar was set up at the coastal village of Tarangambadi about 280 miles from Madras. There was also a Danish settlement at Serampore, near Calcutta where old Danish landmarks are being restored on the Old Danish Road such as the Denmark Tavern. The Danes were more known for their missionary activities there than for commerce. These settlements were perhaps the first cultural forays of the protestant west on India, and it came to involve Germans as well. In June 1801 the Danish were defeated at Tranquebar by the Scots Brigade and in 1845 the whole Danish colony was sold to England. This ostensibly ended the Danish presence in India. However, their use of Indian hardwoods such as teak and rosewood from India and Indonesia in furniture making became a classic mid-century style. Danes also incorporated India's spices into their cuisine.

You can imagine those ancient Danish folks going back to Denmark and describing the sun, the trees, the people. The fort at Tranquebar, the second largest Danish fort (after the one in Denmark of *Hamlet* fame), is being restored with the blessing of the Indian government. The churches established back then are still active and growing, although they are no doubt part of the Church of South India now.

I was talking to a Scandinavian lady about the use of cardamom in Indian recipes, and she said: "Oh, I thought cardamom was exclusively Scandinavian as we use it in many recipes." I laughed and asked if she had ever seen a cardamom tree growing in Sweden—or, a rosewood tree in Denmark? Or teak? Denmark still relies on India and other tropical countries to provide its raw products and spices.

The lovely, exotic cardamom, is said to have been used by Cleopatra in the seduction of Marc Anthony in Egypt. Although Danes began using this ancient spice before their settlement in Tranquebar, the cardamom trees of the south enhanced their love of it. Cardamom, a plant mentioned in ancient Ayurvedic literature, is native to south India and flourishes in the Cardamom Hills of Malabar. These versatile and powerful seeds (from the dried fruit pods) are used in curries in India, to flavor coffee or tea, and to flavor cakes, breads and even schnapps in Denmark. Cinnamon was another spice that the Danish adopted into their culture.

Cinnamon was coveted by the Dutch, who controlled much of its production in Ceylon (Sri Lanka). The Dutch East India Company (VOC, Verenigde Oostindische Compagnie), founded in 1602 and liquidated in 1795, was the largest and most impressive of the early modern European trading companies operating in Asia. They held power in Cochin for over 130 years. Some of their possessions included Cannanore, Tangasseri (near Travancore), Quilon and even Pondicherry for a short time. Dutch surnames among Anglo-Indians include, Hoogwerf, Van Haeften, Van der Reit.

The French East India Company (Compagnie des Indes Orientales) was created for commercial reasons in 1664 and established in India by 1719. The French, under the leadership of Joseph Francois Dupleix, fought against the British, but were defeated by Robert Clive and the company was abolished in 1769. Pondicherry and Chandernagore were still under French control at Indian Independence. They left their names with Anglo-Indian families: La Fontaine, Lefever, Lefebre, DeBeaux and Rocha.

Armenians came to Madras in the early 1600s. There was a large Armenian community in Calcutta, and many emigrated to Australia and England in the late 1940s. My parents' friend, Armen George, migrated to Sydney. He specialized in exporting curry powders and once sent a box of mangoes to the Prime Minister of Australia, my mother says.

Today, in India, an Anglo-Indian is anyone of mixed European heritage (whether it be Dutch, Portuguese, British or French) and Indian. The Victorian racial separateness fostered by Charles Darwin hardly matters anymore. Indian food and habits are more adapted to the climate and landscape. What remain is a name, a song, a story that endures. In New Zealand, Australia, Canada, Britain and the United States, Anglo-Indians gather their collective past to pass on to their children and grandchildren who may view it as a mere curiosity. Those who lived in India—whether for a a few years or for generations, or who may claim to have never inter-married—have children, grandchildren and even great grandchildren who are consumed with interest, filling genealogy research lists as they search for those few enigmatic years their ancestors spent in the sun, under a topi or parasol, living the Raj. The stigma of colonization is not relevant to them. They seek culture more than history.

Anglo-India was not a place, a race, or a time. More than anything, it was a state of mind. It was a political and economic situation that ordinary people lived through. The World Map was at one time covered in pink denoting British dominance. Anglo-Indians now live all over the globe and the Internet is proof that the sun is always shining somewhere on an Anglo-Indian.

The land that Anglo-Indians romanticized for generations was simply an illusion. Once abroad, we had to adjust and to learn anew all that the land of our new home had to offer. In India today the Anglo-Indian community is strong and moves forward to be stronger. People of different Anglo-Indian backgrounds and states now work to gain more recognition and to preserve their original Trusts. The Raj ended. The sun set on the British Empire, but the hundreds of thousands of Anglo-Indians who crossed the Indian Ocean did not disappear. They brought to the world their love of chutneys and curries and hundreds of years of a cuisine that is a unique blend of British, French, Danish, Dutch, Portuguese, and Indian flavors.

12

MY IRISH GRANDMA

Her father came from Blarney,
That's why we talk so much.
Her name was Adelaide
It was her grandfather
A merchant or a coal scuttler,
He came aboard a ship,
A stow-away perhaps?
To find himself in India.
My grandma said she was Irish
And, I believed her.

The soles of my feet are white
Like Irish potatoes, she said,
She was married when she was fifteen
She gave birth on the kitchen table.
He cut the cord for a son, my dad,
In a railway junction town
A place called Katpadi.
Grandma always said she was Irish
And, I believed her.

She had a lover at fifty
A much younger man
Loving her gently he wooed her
Crossing her heart in vain.
When her older husband died,
He was my grandfather, actually.
She married her young lover.
Because she was Irish, she said
And, I believed her.

She was widowed again
But she had spirit,
She grumbled and groused
When things went wrong.
She had pictures of her husbands
In a locket over her heart.
She died loving everyone.
My grandma was really Irish.
That's what she told me
And, I believed her.

My grandmother, my father's mother, was not Irish although she said she was. Her grandfather was Irish, and he married an Indian woman named Mary. My grandmother was an Anglo-Indian.

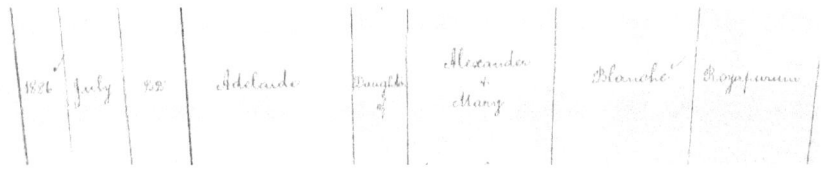

A record of the birth of my grandmother Adelaide Blanche in Royapuram, Madras, 1886.

Adelaide was a strong woman who was instinctive and practical. She took care of us when my parents went on a holiday to England. This is when I learned of her love of the birds and the trees and the little brook that ran in our backyard on Spur Tank Road, in Madras. Together we would watch the flying foxes cross the river late at night. She had a pet parrot who was carried away by an errant cat one day, making her sad and enveloping us children in that cloud of emotion at the loss of a pet. I had an admiration and a bond with her. I visited her often with my dad when we lived in Madras. She always had good stories to tell that I relished. I wish I could remember them all.

Photo of my grandmother, Adelaide, with her cat, grandson and her sister or friend. n.d.

13
ECHOES OF THE RAJ

When a tiger up a tree
Kept you home all day,
A cheetah ran alongside your jeep,
Those were the Raj days.

When a monkey ate your fruit,
Flying foxes circling high,
And the rivers were seeded with trout.
Those were the Raj days.

When porters waited by the train
Willing to carry your trunk,
You spoke in Hindustani.
Those were the Raj days.

When your mother gave you birth
And brought you home in a goda gadi
Incense was burned, to flay mosquitoes.
Those were the Raj days.

When the electricity went off,
The hurricane lanterns came out,
You heard family stories till late.
Those were the Raj days.

When fireflies you kept in a jar
Glowed till they tired all night, with
Gold bees from the tall grasses, too.
Those were the Raj days.

When a furry scorpion could scare you,
Or the Spider Lady make you laugh at the fair,
Gunboat Jack gave a thrill riding high.
Those were the Raj days.

The snake charmer came to call the cobra outside
Elephants trumpeting far away
While the tiger's eyes were burning bright
Those were the Raj days.

When you wore Christmas dresses,
Birthday dresses and uniforms to school,
Played Seven Tiles or caught butterflies
Those were the Raj days.

When a pair of red shoes made you smile,
Time wafted by in frames per week
Not frames per second.
Those were the Raj days.

Memorizing poetry of Wordsworth or Keats,
Freshly ground peanuts, long-simmered jams,
Afternoon tea was the meal of the day.
Those were the Raj days.

Counting the horses by blacks and by whites,
The tropical Sun straight above in the sky
The moon glowing large like it was day.
Those were the Raj days.

A language class in Latin
Left you speaking Double-Dutch,
And that was all that bothered you.
Those were the Raj days.

In those good days, in those old days,
Times remembered, times forgot,
Echoes of life in India, way back.
Those were the Raj days.

Published as "*Memories of the Raj; a poem*" by Joy Chase in Leaf by
Leaf (literary magazine). Evergreen Valley College. Spring 2006
p. 102.

14
A DAY IN THE LIFE OF A MEMSAHIB

Life in faraway India seemed like a hoity-toity time to those Europeans who received letters from their Anglo-Indian relatives and friends. News of large staffs and verandaed bungalows, tiger hunts and summer resorts sounded like the life of the idle rich, which only a few people lived.

Anglo-Indians were often able to have help in their homes, even those of lesser means. The economic inequities, the large population of India and existing cultural patterns made this possible. There did not seem to be a stigma attached and many so-called "servants" were considered part of the family. In turn, they were loyal to the families who employed them. Growing up, I often played with the children of people who worked in our home, and they were my friends. A cook we had in Bangalore had children who were in college and in the same grade as I was. Anthonyama and I always played together, her mother was our cook. A friend of mine more recently has sponsored many of the children of her staff to go to college so that future generations will have more equal opportunities.

Perumal, the lead house staff in Bangalore, was a very efficient and trusted man. He managed the household which included, the driver, the ayah (children's maid), the sweeper (that lowly job of cleaning bathrooms and sweeping floors that was relegated to the lowest of castes), the Gurkha (who guarded the property at night, although we suspected he slept most of the time); the cook (no one really managed the cooks, who had a law of their own); the dhobi (the washer man, who came once a week); the mali (gardener); the chokra or chokri (younger helpers who helped the higher ranked staff with chores). Perumal read the newspapers and gave us the updated news. He was able to send his son to college to help their family move into the middle class. Staff in our households were treated with respect.

To those friends and relatives who lived in England during colonial times, life in India seemed like a mystery, a grand affair filled with unimaginable delights—notwithstanding early deaths from cholera or black fever and even childbirth. Stories of elaborate bungalows, tiger hunts, summer retreats, monsoon rains, blazing heat, important and official guests, and lots of dinner parties fascinated them. Letters written by Anglo-Indians to those "back home" enhanced these views and perpetuated the myth that England was actually still home to Anglo-Indians who had lived in India for generations. My mother continued this habit when I left for America and would not share any negative news of my life with her friends in India. When I broke my leg on a ski trip, it was kept a secret. In fact, I felt very alone and would have welcomed support and news from extended family and old friends in India.

Members of my family have lived in Bangalore for over a hundred and fifty years and that street in Bangalore is named for my great-great-grandfather, Mathew Clapham. Although he married Jane DeBeaux in Madras, he gave his residence as Bangalore. Jane DeBeaux is buried in Bangalore where her children have lived. My great-grandmother known as Lilly, and Patrick Lillywhite were married in Bangalore. Lilly's daughter, Florence, married my grandfather Harry Shepherd in Belgaum, but they lived in Bangalore for many years. My uncle Harry was baptized at Holy Trinity Church at one end of the old South Parade Road on Trinity Circle.

Holy Trinity Church in Bangalore.

My mother, Isabel, was married at the Gospel Hall in Richmond Town. Her brother, my Uncle Len, lived in Bangalore. His son my cousin, Sean Shepherd maintains his residence in Bangalore (although he works in Kuwait) and his children consider it their home. That's six generations and counting. In many cities in India, Anglo-Indians insisted that England was their home—until they emigrated there in the late 1940s and early 1950s and were awakened to the realities of post-War Europe. My Dad's family (the Chase family) has probably lived in Madras for longer and my cousins there continue their residence today.

Higginbotham's Bookstore in Madras with books in English and Tamil available. This photo was taken in 2019.

THE MEMSAHIB

The memsahib was the woman of the house, the owner of the property or the wife of the sahib who was master of the house. These terms are of Arabic and Urdu origin. Sahib and memsahib were given to men and woman for respect like Mister or Mrs. This title became loosely applied to all men and women of European descent during the British Raj. Anglo-Indians were termed this way, and young women were often called Missy. My mother was known in our household as the memsahib and my dad was known as the bara sahib "big master," especially as he rose in the ranks at the bank. When there was more familiarity, especially in the south, the term Ama was used for mother. Recently, I heard the term Akka (big sister) used to respectfully address a young female head of household in Chennai.

Management of the household in that tropical weather required vigilant organization by the memsahib. The day started early when the Lady-Of-the House (who my dad often lightly referred to as the LOH) unlocked the door for the household staff to enter the main house and start the day. In our house, prayer and a bible reading session accompanied morning tea. Afterward, we had breakfast, which started a long preparation for the rest of the day. My mother would go to the pantry or storeroom where she kept dry goods under lock and key. After a discussion of the day's menu with the cook, she would measure out the necessary rice, dal, bean flour, wheat flour and other dry ingredients needed for the meals to be prepared. Sometimes the maître de head of staff would be the only one who spoke English and he would translate to the cook. In a big house, he would have a young boy to help him move the heavy drums or sacks and tins and would measure out the needed items in Indian measures such as a viss, seer, olock, pollum or a teacup in a pinch. She would then get an estimate of what fresh ingredients the cook needed to buy and give him cash, recording the amount in her book in his presence. All the dry goods were then stored back in the pantry, clean and tightly sealed to keep out any insects or rodents. The storeroom was then locked again.

Meals such as an elaborate lunch that usually included curry and rice was either taken or sent to school or work. It was thought that hot, spicy food was better eaten in the middle of the day. Tea was a sustaining meal in the warm afternoon. Dinner was served late, after the day had cooled and the sun dropped below the horizon. In the mornings the shuttered house was opened up and all the doors and windows were kept open all day, except for during the afternoon siestas. It was then closed down each night before the workers left to their own quarters or perhaps to a village on the edge of the town.

Although the British have often been accused of being stuffy and aloof, they could not and did not live in India for three hundred years without incorporating some of its culinary traditions into their own. Sometimes they would wear local dress, which was called mufti, especially as opposed to being in uniform. The idea that Anglo-Indians only ate military rations in India is preposterous. The famous writer, Rumer Godden tells us that they were served chicken pilau and dal in their home in India in 1914.

MORNING TEA AND BREAKFAST

Chota Hazri was a small breakfast, mentioned by Kipling. It means, literally, a small snack. The term has Hindi origins and was commonly used by Anglo-Indians. Porridge was served. Quaker Oats were widely available in India (my mother thought it was the perfect food) and other cereals—rice, ragi (finger millet), sago (usually made from the sago palm but sometimes from tapioca), and cream of wheat. Hot toast and bacon with fried or half-boiled eggs were not served daily. Occasionally, the local egg-hopper woman was paid to come in with her sigri (a small charcoal grill) and her chatties (traditional clay cooking pots) to make a delicious breakfast of rice pancakes, known as hoppers with eggs, served with sweet coconut milk. In Calcutta, a kedgeree was sometimes made with leftover cooked rice and masala-fried fish, cooked in dekshis or pans.

THE LONG MORNING AND LUNCH

My dad would be driven to work by his driver, when he had one, only around ten o'clock. The cook went to the bazaar, carrying the agreed upon list of foods to buy. My mother directed the rest of the household activities. This could include overseeing the Mali for the garden (malis are a sub-caste of a sub-caste and have a long lineage as gardeners), a sweeper to mop and sweep the floors and clean the bathrooms (because of caste considerations, these tasks had to be divided between two cleaners), a maître de (often called a houseboy who helped manage the household) and a dhobi (a washerman who washed our clothes and linens). If the dhobi was overdue in returning our wash from his riverside ghat that led down to a rocky landing by the river, my mother could be sure he had lent out our sheets to his neighbors for a celebration or across town for a wedding. Her white sheets would be used for tablecloths and then washed again before being returned to her. The indelible dhobi marks placed on each item were like a secret code used to reassemble each load after he had collected them and then washed, starched, dried, and folded them before bringing them back to our home. Once a week was washday when the dhobi came to exchange the wash. He dressed in white, with a big bundle of folded clothes wrapped in a double sheet. Wherever the clothes had been in the interim, here they were now, rock-slapped, bleached, sun-dried, rice-water starched and ironed flat with a heavy coal iron. My mother, as her mother and grandmother had done, took out her dhobi book and she and the dhobi started counting. They counted the returned clean wash and the outgoing dirty wash and recorded everything in that book, including what had been lost and any items he was returning that he had not brought back the previous time. Every piece had to be accounted for, even my dad's detachable collars and the handkerchiefs.

While the memsahib, my mother, kept the household organized, interacted with staff, or contracted services, the children (when they were not in school) often played with the children of the service-providers. My mother recalls that their dhobi would bring a donkey along to carry his burden of clean clothes to the house and her brothers would ride the donkey around while their mother and the dhobi counted out the linen. One day they convinced my mother, then probably in her teens, to take a ride on the donkey, swearing that no harm would come to her and promising to watch and help. My mother trusted them and reluctantly got on the donkey. As soon as she sat on it her brothers whipped the donkey. It bolted, knocking her off, kicking her and breaking her wrist. It was an event she has not forgotten.

The cook returned from the market and accounted for every anna spent, which was recorded in a food accounts book. In those days, before decimalization, children memorized their twelve- and sixteen-times tables because twelve pies (or, pice) made an anna and sixteen annas made a rupee. A person who was not quite up to par was said to be "not sixteen annas to the rupee." My father remembered begging his mother for one pie to purchase candy. The cook and my mother would quibble about two annas, going back and forth until they agreed and the change from shopping was correct. With the fresh greens and meat, he had purchased, along with vegetable and bananas, mangoes and coconuts, the cook proceeded to make lunch which was the largest meal of the day. During the week, tiffin-carriers (many-tiered lunch boxes) were filled with curry and rice and side dishes and sent to the sahib at work and to the children at school. The tiffin-carrier consisted of several compartments, each for a specific part of the proscribed meal: rice, a foogarth (fried vegetables with coconut), papadams (light crispy crackers made from rice flour), a vegetable or meat curry and a little pickle or chutney. As children, we loved unpacking our lunches. Sandwiches were for tea, not lunch.

Most times, someone who worked for the household delivered my dad's lunch. My mother remembers paying a woman in Madras who would arrive with a big basket on her head at noon. My mother would fill our tiffins with hot, freshly made curry, rice and foogarths. The tiffin-carrier-woman would have other tiffins in her basket and would have to take a train to deliver all the lunches and then later collect them for a fee. She would eat any remaining food and return the empty tiffins.

However, in Bombay there is an elaborate system of people who deliver lunches all over the huge metropolis. How the complicated exchanges and relays possibly work, with the original owners ending up with their own tiffin, is a wonder to all. The leftover food was often eaten along the return route, and the tiffin-carrier always came home empty. Curry and rice for lunch was an institution among Anglo-Indians, often with a banana and a side of pickle.

THE SULTRY AFTERNOON AND TEA

After lunch, the house was closed down, shutters were pulled, doors locked, and the staff and merchants left for the siesta. Everything was quiet during the heat-drenched afternoon. A monkey might take this opportunity to leap off a tree and steal a plantain (banana) from the kitchen verandah. A stillness and silence fell over the city and even the sahib dozed in his office for a short while during the afternoon siesta.

With less vigor than in the morning, the house reawakened. Everything was opened up again. The sun, less strident with its lengthening rays, cast shadows slowly over the house. Tables were set for afternoon tea. Here we had a marble or Madeira cake, jam sandwiches, buns with Golden Syrup or sweet treacle, scones, biscuits, and sometimes, especially if there were guests, curry puffs, coconut puffs and guava cheese. At Christmas, there was dark plum fruitcake with cul-culs, rosa cruickees (coquese) and black rice doh-dhole halva. Late afternoon tea was always a special time.

THE COOL EVENING

In the pre-twilight after tea, while the children played outside, itinerant entertainers would often drop by. It might be a man and his ox, a "boo madu" who played a deep-toned flute that made a boo-oo sound. He would come to the front of the house with his lean ox (madu is Tamil for cow or ox). Decorated with flowers and colored powders, the ox would bend a knee and bow low. We would all cheer and the man would have the animal perform a sort of dance. Afterwards, my mother would send out a baksheesh tip and they went on their way until their next visit.

Other times, a snake charmer would come from the local bazaar with his special snake-charming flute and his round basket filled with de-venomed snakes, cobras included. Setting the basket down in plain view some distance from the front of the house, he would musically call the snakes halfway out of the basket, and they would bob their hoods back and forth and wave their forked tongues furiously. By what seemed like magic to us, he would charm them back into their basket and, to everyone's relief, put the lid back on. More baksheesh would be sent out, this time more generously. Snake Charmers could be useful. One did not know when a snake charmer might be needed to deal with a snake and get it out of the house. In this case, it was better to have a snake charmer who was kindly disposed towards the family.

Sometimes, a violinist, a bagpiper or a wandering minstrel would stop by and sing or play some old English ditties, collect a tip and be on their way again.

The hawker's visit was most interesting. In the early years of the Raj, hawkers in India were Chinese who had taken a detour off the ancient Silk Road. Before the War and Independence and the fighting on the North East Frontier Area (NEFA), it was always Chinese hawkers who came by our house. They usually came in the morning, and often spent the entire day, pulling out silks, jades, and other treasures they had bought or traded for along the way. It was only after the decline of the Silk Road that the hawkers became local itinerant Indians, traveling north to south and back inside India. The hawker, who often had a helper, brought several bundles of goods. Slowly and methodically, he unpacked every single bundle onto the verandah rugs or living room carpet and displayed the items carefully for the memsahib to view, along with the children and any visitors. There were jade beads, bangles, earrings, and brooches in all colors, some with gold or silver filigree work, silk by the yard or scarves, boxes of all sizes and shapes made of detailed inlaid wood, silver or jade carvings, resins and camphor, nutmegs and cloves. The process of bargaining, bartering, or purchasing items was complex. Prices had to be haggled over and a lively to and fro was established. To barter, my mother had to look around the house for items she might be ready to part with. The hawker was the only one who really knew the value of everything in the microcosm of his World Trade Market. Much to my father's chagrin, my mother once traded some beautiful carved brass vases that were wedding gifts for large glass bottles. Another time, we traded our heavy jade and semi-precious-stone necklaces for plastic pop-beads when that had come into style.

The baker brought the day's order of bread on his bicycle; and when my mother made her twenty-five pounds of dark fruitcake for Christmas, it was the baker who put it in his ovens for four hours to bake it slowly. Everyone in the household got into the mixing of that cake, including the children.

The woman who sold turkeys came with her little flock, chasing them along the road. They were so skinny that it was no wonder they had to be kept for three months to fatten up for the holidays. Ducks were sold this way as well. If you didn't own a cow, a man would come by with his cow and milk it in front of the memsahib. She had to ensure that the milk can was clean and not half filled with water. However, the milkmen were adept at adding water in the blink of an eye. If you did have a cow, and we often owned up to three even in the city, then the milkman would come by to milk our cows. Even the egg man came by and my mother would bring out a big bowl of water and float each egg to see if it was good. A good egg was heavy and would sink to the bottom of the bowl. Occasionally a seamstress or ironing lady would come to do some mending and iron clothes, especially those that were too fine to be trusted to the dhobi. Or an ironing man would come with his coal iron and board and iron your things on the verandah. Many of these services continue in India in different forms. There was never a dull day when you were living the Raj life.

"The past is a foreign country; they do things differently there."

— L.P. HARTLEY, THE GO-BETWEEN, 1953

THE PROPER-ISH DINNER

The burra sahib returned from work around six o'clock in the evening. Many Englishmen were presented with a drink of scotch, by the bearer (not his wife). My dad, however, never drank alcohol so this sequence did not occur in our home. My mother and the rest of the family always dressed up for dinner, changed out of the loose housedresses worn during the hot tropical days. The children were fed early and then played outdoors, supervised by their ayah until it was time to go to bed. Sometimes the sahib and the memsahib were invited out to dinner. In some circles, this would mean going to The Club, but my devoted dad was more likely to attend a bible study or prayer meeting.

Dinner guests arrived at seven or eight. The table was beautifully set with damask or lace tablecloths and serviettes, china, and silver for the many courses, using whatever equivalents the family owned. Water or cool lemon juice was served with the meal. When company was present, the time when drinks were served might expand, with the bearer running back and forth with drinks between the drawing room, where guests awaited dinner, and the kitchen or bar. Whiskey was often the drink of choice of the Raj men, and it was attributed all kinds of healing qualities. Beer was a second choice and a special brew, called India Pale Ale was popular with the troops. Tonic water became an important drink in the mid-nineteenth century—especially with the addition of gin—as it contained quinine, which was used to ward off malaria. Even if the family was tee-totaling as many were, especially in the Victorian Era, people still gathered and got a good feeling from drinking cool soft drinks in jocular company. Guests chatted and exchanged stories until the bearer gave the memsahib the word that dinner was ready. My mother would then go to check on the meal and all the arrangements. When everything was to her satisfaction, she gave the order to ring the dinner bell. Guests entered the dining room and were properly seated by age, gender, rank, and status. The bearer served the food, also according to rank and status, serving the ladies first. He held the dish for the guest to take food and place it on their plate. Sometimes, she had a bell under the table where she sat to call the bearer for the next course or when one was finished to clear the table. Elaborate divisions of a meal were served on occasion with guests—starting with a small appetizer or soup and moving onto a delicate fish dish, then the main entrée followed by dessert. This was not difficult to accomplish with the staff and a chef and many chokras (young boys who worked below him). Consommé, almond soup or a vigorous mulligatawny was served hot, followed by a course of lightly masala-fried fish or fish cutlets with lemon or lime wedges. Next, perhaps a roast of lamb or masala lamb chops, Country Captain (sautéed chicken with chilies) or mutton cutlets with masala-tossed cauliflower, stuffed eggplant with some sliced tomatoes or cold beets. Once my mother was called to the kitchen and was told that the biryani that the cook was making had been ruined somehow, so off a young staffer went to the local shop to buy several packets of biryani, which were secretly served. The cook, nevertheless, got all the praise.

My dad, Stephen Chase when he and my mother, Isabel, took a holiday in England to attend the Maranatha Plymouth Brethren Convention and it coincided with the coronation of Queen Elizabeth II. Taken on the steps of St. Paul's Cathedral in London, 1953.

One of my favorite dishes, growing up in Madras, was mentioned in a Cookery for Anglo-Indian Brides published in London in 1888. They called it Podolong-cai au jus. This book is long out of print. We called this dish Snake cai Curry, cai meaning vegetable. It is like a meat-stuffed zucchini in a curry sauce.

Salads were different from the obsequious chopped lettuce variety common nowadays. In some parts of India salad greens were tender and green, but in the hot plains these were difficult to cultivate. Coarser greens were more readily available, and they would be cut up and lightly sautéed with onions and fresh grated coconut. Lettuce, cauliflower, brussels sprouts, carrots, and cabbages were transported from the hills. I had the task to cut fresh flowers from the garden and arrange them in huge bouquets in vases for the house and to make decorative salads for dinner, a creative outlet that I loved.

Dessert would be a coconut custard, rice or bread pudding or banana fritters. Coconut crepes with sugar and lemon were my favorite. These were Anglo-Indian desserts, neither Indian nor British. After dinner, lightly browned cashew nuts and fresh demitasse Indian coffee was served. Sometimes a board or card game followed.

GOODNIGHT, MEMSAHIB!

After the guests had gone, helpers and servants said their late salaams and the house was locked up. My parents tucked their mosquito nets safely in their four-poster bed, securing them in each corner. The room had, unfortunately, been sprayed with DDT first, a choice among evils. In the distance, as they drifted off to sleep, my parents might hear the mystical sounds of chanting at an ancient Hindu temple or the continuous melodies of an all-night wedding celebration. Jasmine filled the air with a pungent perfume and the faint smell of incense hovered gently. Dawn might bring the sounds of elephants trumpeting and myna birds singing in the mango trees. India was alive. It never left you wishing for sensory detail.

PART THREE
DEEP CONNECTIONS

15

INDIA IN MY HEART

India is in my heart. I can eat dal, rice and spinach any day of the week. I discovered that mung dal is great for the stomach. I remember having dal every day with our curry and rice. The essential essence of India fills my life, from my curtains and tablecloths to other artifacts, wall hangings and art. I can give or attend a Bollywood party and live in Raj style, as I interpret it. My roots manifest in so many ways. I am an American citizen and participate in my right to vote, speak up when necessary and write whatever I wish, invoking our First Amendment right of freedom of speech and the Nineteenth Amendment that gave women the right to vote in this country. Anglo-Indians, whether in India or other countries of the world, follow the laws of the land they are in. Some Anglo-Indians in India have given back to the country of their birth in so many ways including holding office or supporting charities.

As a child I was not involved in the struggle for freedom, but I have read about our great leaders and honor them. I do not in any way endorse, nor do I try to glorify, what the East India Trading Company did in India or the takeover by Queen Victoria that made India a colony of England. These were realities of another time that had negative consequences for unprepared lands. In the end, India solidified and unified to become one country. The results of partition were very sad with families broken apart and lives ended too soon.

I identify with self-rule as promulgated by Mahatma Gandhi and Nehru. I was recently saddened by the venom of a friend of a friend on social media who accused me of being a colonist and having imperial leanings. This is a total misunderstanding of my belief in each person and country to practice self-rule. Perhaps it is a lingering prejudice toward the British and Anglo-Indians from Indians, even now. Stereotypes cling to the bone.

The embers of the Raj life always burn, manifesting itself in many positive ways. Anglo-Indians suffered the fallout of colonialism and were not the rulers. We were originally courted and accepted by the lonely British soldiers and tradesmen, but through the years this led to being ostracized and ousted from ranks in the British Army. In America, too, from that time until after the Second World War there was segregation of the army. Similarly, in India the army was divided into the British Army, the Anglo-Indian Army, and the Indian Army.

By the time I was in college in Madras all of this was gone, India was Independent, and I was hearing stories of "the good life" when the British were there. These tales were well spiced with a mythology of grandeur and happy days. Compared to the wrenching changes that post-war India wrought, it was the past that seemed gay and light, I suppose. It is never easy to be an immigrant, but I carried these feelings of buoyancy and joie de vivre, gleaned from the embers of the Raj, into my new life abroad. It fuels my life still. During days of isolation and social distancing due to the nuevo coronavirus pandemic and the sometimes smoke-filled air from California's wildfires, it is difficult to keep the internal feelings of optimism going. However, being steeped in Anglo-Indian positivity is very helpful.

It was hard to leave India. My family did not strike out immediately after 1947, when many, many Anglo-Indians quickly left with few possessions and much hope, bound for countries where they only spoke the language and could rally around some of the holidays, like Christmas. To many the church was a solace. When I got a scholarship to a small Baptist college in Wisconsin, I was the first from my family-of-origin to leave India. My sister came to the USA a few years later. Then most of the rest of my family immigrated to Australia in the late sixties, while one sister moved to Canada. I found myself automatically driving on the left side of the road in America and had to take a driving course to relearn my driving habits. In the bargain, I learned to park easily anywhere. I did not know how to wash dishes or wash my clothes. I could not cook. But I knew that being Anglo-Indian I would have to try, to learn, to adapt, to take care of myself in every way, however scared I was then and, in some ways, am even now.

I experienced racism and exclusion in the West on occasion. It was not that different from the exclusions we experienced as Anglo-Indians in India from all sides. Geoffrey Moorhouse says in India Britannica "There are ample grounds for suggesting that often far too many of them (the British) were guilty of, in today's jargon, straightforward racism." We belonged but were often thought of as not belonging. These conflicting ideas persist. I belong where I am planted. We are only now coming into an age when "multiracial" is becoming a recognized ethnicity. I do believe that race is a myth perpetuated by social contingencies, and its ramifications in society are evident. In Toronto, I was asked to leave my apartment and move out with only a few hours' notice, but the people I worked with were so kind and helped me in many ways to reestablish my life. In Menlo Park, California, I was denied an apartment because of my perceived race and that of my friends. My desire for an equal society, with opportunity for all, moved me to work in the African American movement in Kenosha, Wisconsin and I took a job as the librarian in charge of a library in East Palo Alto, which had a majority African American population at the time. I wrote and received state grants to promote a special collection of books on Africa and the African American community, which became the beacon for knowledge in this special subject area for the whole county. As Anglo-Indians, we can adapt today, just as we have for 500 years in India.

Life is a moveable feast, as Hemmingway told us, and we are all at the table. Biryanis, fish curries, vegetables galore or only vegetables cooked in so many ways, all at the table. When my California-born children were little, we would have chicken curry for Thanksgiving.

But, as it became evident that they needed to meld into our chosen country, we began to roast a turkey in keeping with American tradition, but accompanied by a nice hot prawn vindaloo to spice up the meal. It is l'amour not de la guerre, for love not war. India remains in my heart.

16

INDIA TO ANGLO-INDIA

I ndia was a thrilling place, a frightening place—a place of conflict both internal and external. It attracted people from all over the world thanks to the fables about its people, its land, and its customs. The Raj endured for a long time and created a community "between." I felt this betwixt-ness growing up in India. My dad convinced me, however, that we as Anglo-Indians got the best of the British and the best of Indian characteristics. I don't know that this is true, but the idea sustained me. It is mostly novelists and movie directors who dramatize an existential conflict, depicting my people as torn between cultures and ethnicities. No further from the facts can this be, as Anglo-Indians in India and abroad seem to relax into both cultures seamlessly.

I was an emerging Indian in a newly independent India without losing my British orientation. I felt the pull to emigrate ten years after Independence. I especially admired Nehru, Mahatma Gandhi, and Indira Gandhi. I read their books and was steeped in the concept of Satyagraha promulgated by Mahatma Gandhi. Satyagraha was derived from Sanskrit and stood for non-violent passive resistance, a policy of insistence on truth by civil disobedience. This concept was taught to

Martin Luther King who embraced non-violence although he died a violent death as did Gandhi. I was impressed, by the concept of a "pen-down" strike, where every worker went to work but refused to do any work by putting down their pens. It was brilliant. The Salt March was a turning point, as were Gandhi's visits to the Lancashire Mills in England. Where did the Anglo-Indian community fit into all this? How would they survive? How would Anglo-Indians be viewed by other Indians when competing for jobs? These were questions that plagued our community and spurred us to make drastic decisions to emigrate or stay at that time.

When I graduated from an international school in Ooty with my Senior Cambridge High School certificate, I stayed in India while many of my classmates went to Australia, Canada, England, and America. I was not at all sure where I should be or what I should do next. We lived in the town of Cochin, and I took some shorthand and typing classes, assuming I would need to work, even though I was reluctant to enter the marketplace.

My mind was on Shakespeare, which I devoured, reading play after play during those long days. We lived in Allepey for a while before moving to Cochin, in an enormous house that shook in the strong Kerala thunder and lightning storms. I knew no one my age in this town. When we moved to Cochin, I met some young officers in the navy, but my parents were over-protective and directive of my life and chaperoned me incessantly. It raised the flight response in me, and I started to think about living abroad to have some freedom for myself. I embarked on this alone.

Soon, my father was transferred again, this time to Madras where I knew many young people who had been in our church or had gone to Doveton-Corrie's elementary school with me. My father had attended this school, too, in the 1930s when it was Corrie's School for boys. Having learned that several of my old friends were in college already, I applied to enter Queen Mary's College in the Madras University. Classes had already begun and I was a month or so late, but the president of the college, Dr. Irawady, interviewed me. She sat on a table cross-legged, as a young maid tended her long hair. I was asked to sit on a chair and answer a few questions about my ambitions. At that time, I still had a strong British accent from having attended an English boarding school, which must have seemed odd. I was admitted to college in a minority seat. India had decided that Anglo-Indians were a "scheduled caste minority" and I was able to get a college seat late that semester that had been set aside as such. This category has been dropped for Anglo-Indians living in India now

My life was starting to take shape, and during the next four years I would find myself living in Vepery with the Wilfred Pereira family after my father was transferred again. Then I moved to the Queen Mary's College dormitory. In those hot tropical days in Madras, we slept in a row on the veranda of the dorms with all the other boarding students. Our view was of the vast Indian Ocean, and we were awakened each day by the cawing of crows. Eventually, I lived in a student-living building at the YWCA, also in Vepery. This is a large rambling bungalow where my great aunt, Dr. Esther Chase, had practiced medicine and adopted her brother's children to raise. It was also the place where I had played as a child in the gardens by the lake. Several buildings had been added on the acres of property, including a student building, a working women's quarters and later, an International Hostel.

The women's hostel at the YWCA in Madras with the lake.

Dad was transferred back to Madras in time for me to graduate, and we lived in the Bank House known as Red Craig in Egmore near Numbabakkam. At first, I took a train and a bus to get to Queen Mary's College, past Parry's Corner. Later, I would drive my dad's Triumph, dropping him off at the State Bank of India's statuesque red building on First Line Beach on my way. The State Bank building was designed in the Indo-Saracenic style that British architects invented to blend their English sensibilities with the local Hindu-Islamic culture although it had hints of Buddhist and animist aspects to it. I was one of only two or three students at Queen Mary's who drove a car at the time. I majored in English Literature and took courses in Shakespeare, Milton, and the Social History of England. This was completely out of context with the country I was living in, and so I immersed myself in some self-education. Rabindranath Tagore became my favorite poet and I read his *Gitanjali* over and over as a meditation for many years. He wrote:

> Day by day thou art making me worthy of the simple, great gifts that thou gavest to me unasked—this sky and the light, this body and the life and the mind—saving me from perils of overmuch desire. — Rabindranath Tagore. Gitanjali Revised Edition of Original Version

Queen Elizabeth II of England visited Madras during the time I was at Queen Mary's College. Crowds came out to get a glimpse of this Semai ke Rani, England's Queen. I went with a friend, and we were pushed and pinched by the men in the crowd. There was no possibility of transportation because of the throng. We walked for miles until a kind man, who knew my parents, got us out of the crowd, found a rickshaw for us and told the rickshaw-wallah to take us home. We did see the Queen, however.

I applied to immigrate to Australia. Several of my friends had moved there, including my high school boyfriend, and it seemed to have a friendlier climate than England. I was interviewed by the Australian High Commissioner and given the green light. The only hitch was that he needed to interview my whole family. Australia had a White Policy, which was Euro-centric at that time. My mother and sisters and brother were interviewed some months later in Bangalore, but my dad was away on business. Then, through a friend of my dad's, Robert Frykenberg, I obtained a scholarship to attend a college in America and my life took off in another direction. Robert Frykenberg's parents, Eric, and Doris Frykenberg, were missionaries in India who became friends and mentors to my parents. My brother and I were given names to honor these missionaries who were an early influence on my dad's life.

My awareness of being an Anglo-Indian never faltered, but it was hard to explain to people who had never heard of my community and did not know that we existed. It was difficult for me to understand why people would think that the British could live in India for 300 years and not be intermarried or mixed with the Indian people. It seemed incongruous to me. It still does.

Receiving a prize for my kadhi dress at the All India Handloom Exhibition in Madras, 1960.

Who were the Anglo-Indians? What did they accomplish? How did they become a community? What were their special cultural indicators, their traditions, and their foods? These are questions I have spent my life trying to answer. And even before we were Anglo-Indians, there were the Portuguese and other races that entered our cultural, ethnic stream. We know of a DaCosta family that my family married into who were Sephardic Jews and we are still tracing these influences. We really are a 500-year-old community and family. Anglo-India!

Graduation from the University of Wisconsin, Madison in 1966

17
WORLD WAR TWO

"Seventy-five years ago, Uncle Eddie (James Edward Mathew Shepherd) landed on Sword beach as part of the first wave of the D-Day landings with the 1st Battalion of the Royal Norfolk regiment. He was later awarded the Military Medal during the Normandy campaign for outstanding bravery. Sadly missed, a lovely gentleman and a genuine hero."—John Greg Bryant, my first cousin, in 2019.

A few years ago, I was driving past the Regatta Hotel on George Street in Brisbane, Australia when I had an epiphany. I wondered why the diaspora of Anglo-Indians had occurred. Although I had gone over this in my mind many times, I suddenly awoke as history poured itself into my spirit and I felt a deep sadness.

The Regatta Hotel has its own history, having contributed to liberation when a feminist, Merle Thornton, and her friend chained themselves to the bar to protest its anti-women policy. My friend and I had been asked to sit outside on the patio to have a beer in the 60s. Fast-forward fifty years and it is now Merle's Bar. I felt an emotional connection to this place. It made me think of my own roots. It made me think of our struggles. As I thought about my Anglo-Indian community, I wondered again why we had left our homes in such haste in the 1940s and 1950s, and why my parents moved to Australia with my brother in the late 1960s. It struck me that this was the result of the Second World War.

The State Bank of India in Ooty

War pulls communities apart, changes the course of history, and reverses and zigzags the paths of individuals who land in unexpected places, trying to keep their balance. Following WWII—and because of that war—Anglo-Indians were scattered across the world. England was bankrupt, the losing winners. Rations were the norm in post-war England; and here we came, thinking that this was our home. There had been very little bombing in India. My family lived in a quiet hill town known as Ooty. I remember the day my dad came home in the middle of the day to tell my mother: "The War is over!" but I was too young to remember the horrors of the War. I only saw the scars.

My mother's brothers—Harry Roslyn, Eddie, Lionel and Lenny Shepherd, her brother-in-law (my uncle)—George Welsh and my dad's cousin—Maxwell Chase were in the British Army, Royal Navy and Royal Air Force. Many had lifelong careers in the British Armed Forces. My Uncle Eddie Shepherd was honored with a Military Medal, awarded by King George VI for his bravery at Dunkirk. My Uncle Len was young when he joined the British Army, but he marched back to

India from Rangoon after the war was done. They all joined the army in India. After 1903, there were two divisions of the army of India: The Indian Army was local and permanently based in India together with expatriate British officers and Anglo-Indians (although there was a separation even within its ranks between Anglo-Indians and Indians). The British Army in India consisted of units posted to India that would be returned to the UK after a tour of duty. WWII had a huge impact on the Anglo-Indian community.

My grandfather, Harry Shepherd, had been in the Norfolk Rifles (later called the Norfolk Regiment) in the British Army from the time he was 15 or 16 (having claimed to be 18 to enlist) and was decorated in the First World War (WWI). He was from Trowbridge, England and originally came to India with the British Army. While he was stationed in Belgaum, he met and married my grandmother on the trust. The 'trust' at that time meant that he was marrying a woman who had proven she was British. In fact, my grandfather's supervising officer simply looked at my grandmother and stated that it wasn't necessary for her to prove she was English.

My grandfather took his older sons, Harry, and Eddie, to Jubbulpore around 1936 to enlist them in the British Army in India. This was allowed because he was a bona fide British veteran of that unit. Others may have joined the Anglo-Indian regiments in the Indian Army. After the war, my uncles were repatriated to England, where they married, had children, and carried on like they had always lived there. However, when my grandfather's regiment was repatriated, he decided to stay in India.

After the war and Indian Independence, most Anglo-Indians left India. Those of us who stayed on were able to succeed in the new India in many ways. Everyone who left was "doing well", and they never wrote to complain. We didn't hear about the cold, icy winter, the rations in England after the war, the prejudice, the difficulty getting jobs at the level they were trained, the back-breaking physical work that they were unaccustomed to. Anglo-Indians are not given to complaining. This is just the way it is and was, and there was nothing to be done about the situation except move on, and move on they did, admirably.

In India today, the Anglo-Indian community is as strong as ever. People like Barry O'Brien, Joseph Galstaun, Dr. Beatrix D'Souza, Denzil Atkinson, Alfie DeRozario, Denzil Godin and many, many others deserve kudos for working tirelessly on behalf of the community of Anglo-Indians in all the states, to seek a fair and safe life for the Anglo-Indian community in India.

Beatrix D'Souza, PhD. (Served in the Tamil Nadu legislature and the 12th Lok Sahba. Pres-founder of Forum of Anglo-Indian Women.) With the author, 2019.

18

AN END TO AN ERA

The Raj era was slipping away. In fact, it was gone but its embers glowed. Growing up in Madras, Bangalore, Hyderabad, Calcutta, and Cochin in the late 1950s, I knew the Raj was over. I thought of myself as intrinsically Indian, but there was still a longing, a nostalgic throwback to what seemed like a glorious time for the British in India, and for Anglo-Indians. There had also been mass murders, prejudice, and exclusion, imagined superiority and undeserved feelings of inferiority. Sir Henry Gidney advised, "if there is one thing which you must completely eradicate from yourselves, it is the retention of superiority and inferiority complexes; and you should bring about their replacement with a complex of equality." Anglo-Indians had invented and reinvented their community over and over again. We survived. We still survive; and that is the essence of our happiness. Our joy in living is a quality that is nearly impossible to stamp out of our clan. It has persisted, whether we lived in railway colonies or cities, as we took on various ways and means to live, and whether we were Roman Catholic or Church of England.

I hope we can pass this attitude on to future generations, whether they are the new blend of Anglos in India, or the cricket players and singers, the hard-working immigrants or the new generation who hardly know us, scattered in foreign countries all over the world. Just this one thing that we learned from our ancestors: life is good. Anglo-Indians have an indescribable capacity for enjoying life, knowing life, embracing life, and feeling truly alive.

I was there at Independence, the freedom at midnight from the British Raj. The Raj era had lasted 300 years, from the time the East India Company began trading with India and had its own militia to protect its indigo industry and paid in silver. The Portuguese, the Dutch, the French came before, and later the British were trying to survive in another time with different mores, but there are no excuses.

It was an exciting day, that first Independence on August 15, 1947. My dad had a black Ford V8 on which he had fixed a nameplate that said "Jehu" who was noted in the Bible as driving furiously. He made this plate by melting down old metal toothpaste tubes, casting the molten metal in a mold of sand and polishing it when it was set. We piled into this car and drove into the streets of Madras. Every building was lit up—the Rippon Building, the Imperial Bank of India, Moore Market, Central Station, and other grand buildings some named for governors and note-worthy gentlemen and ladies of the Raj. In the next fifty years most of these buildings would be gone, torn down to make way for new buildings, burned to the ground, like my memory-filled Moore Market, or reappropriated by other means. For some, as in the case of the beautiful Indo-Saracen Victoria Memorial, a photograph reminds in the current concrete textiles shop on Mount Road. The bank, now the State Bank of India headquarters, remains. Although a wall surrounds it, it remains a grand and majestic building on First Line Beach near the harbor.

On that first night, we were caught up in the excitement of the future for a free and self-determining India. We gave no thought as to what would happen to the Anglo-Indian community. As it turned out, hundreds of thousands of Anglo-Indians fled the shores of India, most by passenger boat, seeking a new life in England, Canada, Australia, or America. Their protected jobs in the communications industries of the railways, telegraphs and post offices were reassigned to local Indians, who did not care about the now-deposed British or their quasi progeny, the Anglo-Indians.

Time was moving on, but Anglo-Indians carried their essential natural buoyancy with them wherever they went. As those P&O steam liners pulled out of Bombay, their foghorns blowing a sad goodbye, Anglo-Indians took comfort in each other's company. They sang the old songs and played their guitars on the decks as they sailed farther away from their homes, to lands they knew only in stories.

We carried precious little with us, save the spices in our blood and our grandmothers' recipes in our heads. Remember them, we did: Mutton glacé, Country Captain Chicken, sweet chutneys, and hot vindaloos. These we recreated as best we could, holding tight to those good memories.

My parents chose to "stay on." Dad still worked at the State Bank, previously the Imperial Bank of India, the halls of which I often frequented. Not much later, I received a scholarship to a college in Minnesota in the U.S.A. and flew away carrying the myths and stories of Tamilnadu with me.

My dad had premonitions and strong experiences that he related to me. He told me of a time when he saw a man crazily shaking his whole body in a frenzy and he went up to the man and said: "In the name of Jesus, leave this man." and the man stopped and was still. Such was the power of his word. In America, I had a prescient experience while I was talking to some dorm friends at the time of my cousin Barry's death. I very strongly and loudly heard the funeral bells of an Indian street procession outside the window. So strong was it that it drew me to the window to look out. I was shaken by this experience and went to my room for a while. It was not till many weeks later that I heard that Barry, my cousin and Len's son, had been hit by a truck and died when riding on his motor scooter in Madras.

There was darkness in our lives in India and abroad, but somehow, we always had a glimmer of hope. I lay this down to our Anglo-Indian roots. Through all the indignities and injustices, we had experienced in India such as the trials my parents and their friends called the "Anglo-Indian problem" when I overheard their late-night discussions, it was never one of complete despair.

"There is a gentle warmth in the people...they have a certain confidence and attitude in their body language, which is so much a part of the Anglo-Indian identity."

— DILEEP PRAKASH, SLICE OF LIFE EXHIBIT IN CHENNAI IN THE INDIAN EXPRESS, 2006

19
BEFORE THE DAWN

Before the Dawn
This sterile place
This barren womb of trials
This place of no art or poetry
This place where dogs are dead
God's creatures banned
Children cry, and babies are swallowed up
Love is a word one cannot say
Friendship is misconstrued
Lost, in an impotence of words.
The darker night claims the darkest place
that burns my soul
As my abode.
Do I wait upon permission
To gaze upon the dawn
When light replaces dark?
The dawn must come
Just wait.

First published in the Evergreen Valley College, San Jose literary magazine, Leaf by Leaf, 2012, page 43.

PART FOUR
THE AFTERMATH AND BEYOND

20

GOING TO AMERICA

I felt desolate traveling to America alone in 1963. I did not leave with the boatloads of Anglo-Indians who left India after Independence in the late 1940s and early 1950s. I was missing the storied singing on the decks and camaraderie. I was the first in my immediate family to come to the West. I had a scholarship to a private college for a year, having completed my BA from Queen Mary's College at the University of Madras. I was helped by my parents' friend, Robert Frykenberg, a professor at the University of Wisconsin and son of missionary Eric Frykenberg. Jacob Bouw, my sponsor, met me when I arrived and settled me in an empty dormitory in freezing cold Nyack, New York, 30 miles from New York City. We drove there in the middle lane, frightening for someone who had never been on a freeway before. Jacob Bouw's lady friend read every billboard from New York to Nyack, except those that promoted alcohol or cigarettes which she declared shameful. I was also sponsored by my friend Gwen's husband, Larry Sieck. They had guaranteed my stay in America with a letter to the Immigration and Naturalization Services, I was and still am very grateful.

The security officers who looked at my passport and accepted the x-ray of my lungs, that I was required to carry, complimented me on speaking very good English. I had never been told that I spoke my mother tongue well because it had been a given. No one in England told me I spoke good English, perhaps they expected that in 1963. I was excited to be in America, but I was alone and had no one to share my excitement with. My sponsor and his friend were much older than me and I realized I could not share my wonder and excitement with them. I was wearing a white blouse and my Sunday uniform from boarding school, a pleated grey woolen skirt. I shivered as it struck me that I had left home, probably forever. I'd left my friends from grade school, my sisters and brother, my parents and cousins, my dog. I had, in fact, left India forever. I met up with my friend Gwen and the Siecks later in Rolla, Missouri. I only returned to India fifteen years later for a short visit after my parents had immigrated to Australia. It was six years before I saw them in Brisbane, Queensland on a leave from my job.

I had originally applied for immigration to Australia, so my life was turned around as I found myself going to America instead. Leaving India, I went by train from Madras to Bombay with my mother. My father was already in Bombay for business. Our train had a coal-fired engine, and it took us a few days to complete the trip. Shortly after I went through London and New York, I was in St. Paul, Minnesota and I saw the same type of engine in the main section of their train station as a relic on display. It felt like I had travelled a hundred years in time as well as a long distance. I was ten thousand miles away from home.

Anglo-Indians dispersed worldwide after Independence, most traveling in groups to Canada, Australia, New Zealand, and the British Isles. Few came to America, and it was many years before I was able to locate any Anglo-Indians in the United States.

Traveling to America I was allowed only $20 USD and 2 British pounds. I brought one suitcase weighing 40 pounds, and a tightly packed handbag that weighed about 15 pounds. I wore my delicately tooled Shantiniketan high-heeled sandals the whole way. They were tooled at an arts institute which had been started by Rabindranath Tagore and his father.

When I spent those first couple of nights in New York, I was very alone. Late at night a couple of students also stayed at the dormitory where I stayed, but they were not very friendly. I realized that I had embarked on a journey by myself and would continue alone, although my father had precipitated it.

My United States citizenship certificate (with #s erased for safety) 1980.

I came to the Midwest where I attended Bethel College in St. Paul for a year. In those dark brick and stone buildings, I slept against a wall that was freezing cold in winter. I sneaked into the lounge to get warmer but was soon found out and told to return to my bunk bed by the cold wall. There were kind people, too, who donated warm clothes to me to wear while I studied American Literature. President John Kennedy was shot and killed two months after I arrived. I did not hear often from my family in those days before Internet connections. Malcolm X was shot two years later. Martin Luther King and Robert Kenned were killed after I had been in America only five years. The Vietnam War was raging, and protests and the draft were prevalent.

The next year I received another scholarship and a house fellowship at the University of Wisconsin in Madison. Some couples I met thought I'd make a good babysitter so they could go out on weekends. I was too afraid to babysit, to tell the truth. In the 1960s, most Midwesterners thought pepper was too spicy to add to food. They had very specific rules about which dishtowel to use for various dish-drying activities and I was totally confused. I retreated into myself and watched and waited. I finished my course at Bethel College and applied to graduate school. I had completed my bachelor's degree in Madras and done a bracket year studying American and World Literature and now I wanted to get an advanced degree in Literature, but it was not in the cards. I realized that my Indian degree was not as acceptable for that field and nor would I have been able to bridge the divide between a student visa and a residence in America. At the time, the most coveted and accepted degrees to stay on after a student visa expired were in medicine, engineering and teaching or librarianship. Libraries were always a love of mine. I remembered spending hours in the beautiful library at Queen Mary's College where I climbed the bookshelf ladders up three tiers to find the stories about the Trobrianders written by Margaret Mead or the novels of Daphne DuMaurier like Frenchman's Creek set in Cornwall. I applied to attend the University of Wisconsin Library School graduate program and received my master's degree. It has been a very satisfying career, even with all the changes and moves to mostly digital content. I have enjoyed working in public libraries such as the Kenosha Public Library in Wisconsin and the San Mateo County East Palo Alto branch library in California where I was able to procure grants to create innovative programs. After taking a break when my children were young, I worked over twenty years for a Community College Library in San Jose and still work there as an associate librarian.

All this was not easy, drop that fantasy. I was alone and felt foreign, in spite of interesting male partners and good women friends. It took ten years before I really felt American, and my children still remind me that maybe I'm not. I have a vocabulary larger than many other people. This vocabulary has grown because of having to live in a country that uses a different word for everything I grew up knowing.

For a time at the beginning, I used a Sears Catalog as a reference constantly because it was easier to find a visual of an item. I wanted to figure out the American equivalent for example, a monkey wrench was just an adjustable spanner and anticlockwise became counterclockwise, biscuits were crackers, the boot of a car was a trunk. Not to mention all the Tamil words and some Hindi words that were rattling around in my head. There were all the antiquarian ways we acted or believed to be polite such as men standing up when a woman entered the room or took their hands out of their pockets when speaking. Some of it came from the nineteenth century where education in India had been stuck for some time. Oh, and there was driving on the other side of the road. I had to take driving lessons to get this right.

After I got my master's degree in Library Science, I worked in Wisconsin for a few years. I was not involved in the anti-war movement, but I did volunteer to teach English as a Second Language (ESL) using the Laubach method of associations for which I had taken a course. I also became involved with the African American movement which later extended to my work in East Palo Alto. At the time, this was a high crime neighborhood, and I had my keys stolen which resulted in the library being vandalized and another time a gang of young men came down to the library with tire irons in their hands forcing me to close the library for the safety of the patrons and staff. Eventually my home was broken into, and I was raped, and my collar bone broken. My dreams and most of my feeling safe flittered away in the process. It was a tough job, but I was also able to start art programs for children with volunteer artists, showed films for the locality that I rented from the University of California at Berkeley, and got grants to purchase a minibus to serve outlying neighborhoods in pockets of the under-served. We began a library program for the county jails. The unique collection of books I had put together on Africa and African American literature was called on regularly to answer reference questions.

After my sister came to America, I found a job in California, but not in the city where she lived. I did not hear from friends in India, and I depended on my mother for news. I had no addresses or information on peoples' movements. Once I asked for a recipe and received the weights and measures in viss and olok which were still used in Tamilnadu. In time, though, I made a few good friends. I rely on my friends now and they make the core of my family. I am happy in the cottage I own in the San Francisco Bay Area. When I first came to America, most people had no idea where Madras was and did not know what an Anglo-Indian was. I identified as Indian anyway, so I went with that and stopped trying to explain 300 - 500 years of Anglo-Indian history—500 if you go back to the first Europeans who settled on our shores, or to Vasco da Gama who arrived from Portugal in 1498.

It took a long time to get over the loneliness and trauma of leaving home and to make it in a new country where I had no stakes and no family. My children are not Anglo-Indians but can claim an Anglo-Indian mother. I try to pass down the spirit that all Anglo-Indians somehow manage to maintain. I write about it in my poetry. The light of dawn brings hope. My two daughters are my rock now and they sustain me. I am always searching for my true home. As the famous British actor Peter Ustinov once said, "I feel at home everywhere but not at home anywhere." Although after almost sixty years, I do feel that the United States of America is now my home. The world is my home.

21

EMBERS REIGNITED

I was never completely happy about my given name although it denotes joy. I thought it too short and unimaginative. My mother assures me that she had given it to me because she was so happy at my birth. I thought that I should have a longer name and sometimes called myself Josling Chokalingam in play. I thought that this name had more gravitas. It also projected my British and Indian roots in a nom-de-plume unlike my given names. Later, after I had read a novel I loved at the time, I renamed myself Zonya. This was a Russian name after the protagonist in the book whose title and author I have forgotten. I tried to pass it on to my daughter, but, in negotiation with her father, we settled on Natala, a name I loved, too. I named my second daughter Sheila, a name both Irish and Indian, another name I loved and had positive associations with. I still call myself Zonya when I go online incognito, more recognizable as time goes by. Zonya Chokalingam, maybe (no offence to Mindy and others who own the surname).

Living the Raj life was so much more than history. It was a fantasy —always a fantasy. The style of many colonial houses in India was described by William Hodges in 1781 in Madras. He described them as having long colonnades, open porticoes, and flat roofs. A friend of mine tried to recreate a colonial house in Sacramento, California, just to feel that spaciousness and to hold on to memories.

I remembered the happy times we had around Christmas and the New Year in India. After Armistice Day on November 11, we would start practicing carols for Christmas performances. About a month before Christmas, we would decorate with a frenzy. Every part of our house was decorated. Handmade poinsettias and holly with berries were made new each year, and chains of crepe paper were hung from the high ceilings in the living room coming to the center from every side. Christmas brought cooler weather, and this was welcome. Sometimes choirs—either impromptu or belonging to church choirs— would go to the homes of members and friends, singing carols at each home.

When I came to America, I tried to recreate some of the culture from my childhood. However, it was hard to do almost everything myself. No one seemed to enjoy eating fruitcake and I would end up eating pounds of it over the holidays. Cul culs or Rosie Cookies, which are Anglo-Indian traditional Christmas treats were difficult to make and not cherished by people who were unfamiliar with them. I decided on one tradition, which my family keeps. I make crab curry for New Year's Day. Crab is the best price at this time, easily attainable and delicious. It is a hot, fiery vindaloo curry served with yellow rice and yogurt mixed with tomatoes and onions. You have to eat it with your fingers to get the total sensory experience. Our hankering for India is endless. Although we make our way in other countries, learning to love new cuisines, we often crave that special dish or place where we grew up.

There were Anglo-Indian clubs like the Tolygunj in Calcutta and the Bowring in Bangalore. The Gymkhana clubs began in the 1860s and held competitions in obstacles and rickshaw races, but they soon deteriorated into snobby hangouts for English ladies with their prejudices and exclusivity. However, after Independence the clubs continued as places for networking and sports, like swimming and tennis, with membership open to all who could afford the price. Ooty Club is another famous club where the game of snooker was invented. Anglo-Indians have opened clubs at their post-war destinations where they can congregate, like the Anglo-Indian Center in Perth, the East West Centre in Melbourne, and others. These serve the same purpose as the Railway Clubs did in small towns in India—to bring people together and to remember the good times with old and new friends.

Life is not always easy. The coronavirus pandemic of 2020 begs comparisons with tropical diseases and death in the past. Sir William Book Leishman was a British physician who studied tropical disease in India around 1890. He discovered a protozoon to be the disease agent for kala-azar, which is also known as Black Fever. This fever is said to have caused the deaths of 750,000 people around 1824. He later developed a vaccine against typhoid fever.

Life may not be the party we hoped for, but while we're here we should dance.

— JEANNE C. STEIN, BLOOD BOND

22

A FAMILY WITH FIVE FLAGS

Our first full family Christmas together in twenty-five years was in 2001. We met for my mother Isabel's 80th Christmas. Her birthday was in February, but since my sister was the only family member who could be there on that day, we decided to have a reunion at Christmas in her honor. Our siblings had not been together since our beloved Dad, Stephen Chase, had gone to glory almost ten years before. Now we had our children with us. We could fly five flags. My sister had immigrated to Australia to be with my parents many years earlier, but her son had been born in Toronto, Canada. Her husband Gaston had died. Tim carried a Canadian passport at the tender age of three months. Margo was married to Sam, a great guy from Northern Ireland. My brother, Eric, had immigrated to Australia with my parents at the young age of ten, but he lived in New Zealand with his Australian wife and their daughters —Holly, Jemma, and Miranda—who did the Hakka for us. They were kiwis.

I had been the first to leave India in 1963, traveling alone to the United States of America. There I remained alone, without immediate family, even after my sister, Jen, came to California. I was in Madison,

Wisconsin working on a master's degree, and it was six years before I was able to get a job in California and live a few cities away from her.

The 50th Wedding Anniversary of my parents in Brisbane, Australia.1989. L-R my brother Eric, myself, my dad and mum, my sisters Jenny and Margo.

There we were. The four adult children of my mother, Isabel, and either through domicile, marriage or citizenship flying five flags: Australia, the United States of America, New Zealand, India (once an Indian always an Indian) and the Union Jack. My mother had revoked her long-held British citizenship for Australian. Nevertheless, the Raj still lived inside her. All her siblings had left to live in England in the late 1940s. And, there was Sam, from Northern Ireland. Here we were together, and that was what was important. It was difficult to obtain all the flags, so we let that go.

Let the cooking begin! We were thrilled to have "face time"—to actually look at each other's faces as we talked, chatted and caught up. This was something we could not do on email, instant messaging, or Skype (later Zoom). Most of our children were with us: Natala, Sheila,

Jasmine and Joslyn were Americans. Holly Jemma, Miranda, Sam's son Sammy and my brother's older daughter, Jasmine had all been born in Australia. We all had different Christmas traditions by now, but the tree was there, common to all Western Christian cultures. We had a succulent Australian ham for dinner and added some curries for old times' sake.

During the week or so we were together, we each made sure our favorite dishes came to the table: hot and spicy crab curry; vegetable kormas laden with coconut milk; yellow rice made in a cooker; cabbage fougarth, my mother's specialty (among many others) and dark fruitcake. There were other Anglo-Indian Christmas foods that we may have added—cul culs, hulvas, Dho Dhol (made with black Burmese rice), rosa cuikees, (rosie cookies) OT (the teetotalers drink made mostly from chilies and ginger), Xmas pudding (with money in it) and other items remembered from times long past. Our children remembered none of these but were intrigued by our memories all the same. Although some of us had tried to keep these food items alive, none of us had married Anglo-Indians. Mince, which is ground meat to Americans, is a fragrant chopped delight of preserved fruit that the British put in pies or cakes and that we loved in India. In larger pieces, with the addition of a few good mango chunks and sultana raisins, it made a great chutney.

Back to our *Five Flags* Christmas... Summer in Australia, especially in Queensland, is hot—as hot as a summer in India. Christmas in December in India was always warm, unless you happened to live up in the hills somewhere or in the north. Pine trees were hard to come by in India and I remembered that we used a croton plant once. Its brightly colored leaves hardly needed any decorations. Mostly though, I remember the childish excitement of procuring a tree. There were no Christmas tree lots. Once, we had the mali cut down a huge branch way up high of a casuarina on the beach in front of our house in Cochin. Other times we would drive the car for miles to a casuarina farm out of town, cut down a small tree and take it home on the roof of the car, carefully tied down with jute twine.

One year my friend, Wilfred, had the task of finding a Christmas tree for the family while his mother was busy making the traditional

Christmas halva Dho Dhol with black rice from Burma and Cul culs with coconut milk-laced dough curled on the back of a fork, deep fried and covered with sugar. She also made dark English fruitcake and Rosie Cookies, with a rose-shaped iron dipped in a special batter.

Wilfred and his friend, Freddie, had seen some trees by the Adyar River in Madras so they drove out to that area. They couldn't find a saw, so decided to just hammer a bunch of nails in a line into the tree and then break it off at the trunk. There were many large estates by the Adyar River, some with grand staircases leading down to the river. However, the trees they wanted were far from a big house and they walked around to select a tree. There was a man standing near the tree and, thinking that he might be a caretaker for the trees, they asked his permission to cut down a tree, at which point the man asked for a bribe and disappeared.

As the sun went down and the night began crawling in, they started getting jittery as they hammered in their nails. Freddie thought he heard something. Wilfred said he heard a low growl. They thought they saw a cougar. Their breath grew shallow, and they froze. Just then the tree keeled over, hacked by their jagged row of nails. Before they knew it, a man jumped on them and grabbed Wilfred. Another grabbed Freddie and yelled "chor" meaning "thief." Several men pushed them forward, towards a clearing where they could see a very large white house. They noticed that all the men wore uniforms banded in gold.

Wilfred and Freddie were presented to a small man with large whiskers. He was wearing gold-embossed Turkish slippers but was otherwise very casually dressed. Wilfred immediately recognized him as the Maharajah of Porbandar who maintained a residence in Madras. His Highness' full name was Lieutenant-Colonel Maharaja Rana Shri Sir Natwarsinhji Bhavsinhji Sahib Bahadur of Porbundor. His adopted son went to the private Anglo-Indian school that Wilfred attended, and he had once seen the Maharajah with the prince. This was obviously before the princely purses were ended by the Indian government, which also ended some of the lavish lifestyles of Indian royal families. The Maharajah's pet cougar was tied to a pillar on the veranda, wearing a gold studded collar, seemingly disinterested. The

Maharajah clapped his hands and ordered tea, then gave them an hour-long lecture on honesty and property rights before dismissing them—but not before Wilfred pluckily asked for the tree. The Maharajah magnanimously got his guards to tie it onto the roof of their car saying he had no need of dead trees on his land and wished them and their families a Happy Christmas. That was how Wilfred and his family happened to have the Maharajah's tree for Christmas that year.

HH Maharajah Rana Saheb Shri Bhavsinghji Madhavsingji Baghadur of Porbandar est. 1120. Father of Natwarsingji. (Photo credit indiarajputs.com)

My brother, Eric decided to give a crab curry feast for his friends in Brisbane and we all helped. He held it at a friend's place, not far from the center of town. It looked as though it was in the Australian bush, with lots of verdant greenery around. He rented cookers and bought at least fifty big crab, which he cracked, cleaned, and sautéed with bottles of fresh Vindaloo paste and cans of unsweetened coconut milk. It was delicious, and his Australian friends loved it, too. We made sweet-smelling basmati rice to go with it and side dishes galore. It really was a feast, but the best part was yet to come. Eric's friend, a high-caliber vegetable and fruit vendor, provided us with cases of the best mangoes ever. I still have visions of all those good mangoes that we sliced and ate with ice cream. I hid a case for Mum to eat and savor slowly over the next few days. All of this went well with the inimitable Bundaberg Rum that is unavailable anywhere else. My parents were teetotalers even in India, and my mother still is, but the non-alcoholic Bundaberg ginger beer is pretty good, too.

My dad, Stephen Chase, wearing his "maharajah shoes" and when he graduated from Fuller Theological Seminary in Pasadena, California with an MA.

We each contributed to the milieu on Christmas Day. My adult daughters brought gifts: from Natala, a CD of the old favorite songs, garnered via interviews with all of us. It's a Long Way to Tipperary for Mum; Elvis' Love Me Tender for me; Hit the Road, Jack for my brother; Waltzing Mathilda for the Aussies; and God Save the Queen. Well, that was a bit over the top; California Gurls by David Lee Roth for the California girls, who stood up and sang it with actions; We Are Family for all of us; and the Jana Gana Mana, of course. My sisters, Margo and Jenny and I stood up and sang that last one by heart, having memorized it when India became independent fifty years before. "Jana-gana-mana-adhinayaka, jaya he; Bharata-bhagya-vidhata." Victoriously, we wrapped it up with "Jaya he, jaya he, jaya he; Jaya jaya jaya, jaya he!" ending on the high note because to go down after that would be to show defeat, or so they said. My brother-in-law, Sam was very impressed. "I always wondered if you were true Indians," he said, "but now I know you are!" "Anglo-Indians!" we chorused.

Anglo-Indians. As a child, we were taunted with songs mocking our mixed heritage. "Missy, missy lul" they'd sing as we rode by, high in our rickshaws on our way to school. Our children don't really know what it is to be Anglo-Indian and when we are gone there will be few like us ever again. Hundreds of years of inter- and intra-marriage is taking on a new meaning and a new shape. It can only continue to exist if those of us who remember write it down, say it aloud, and honor the memory of those who have gone before. It is written on our hearts. It is who we are, wherever we live now, whatever we think we are now, whatever the passport we carry says. That too, is who we are.

My daughter, Sheila, a professional photographer, gave us calendars to remind us of India and ourselves. Jasmine (Jenny's daughter) told us of her student world travels, including visiting cousins in Madras. My brother and his wife, Marg, did a skit that my parents had done for years. Margo performed a song that I found after much research for my mother, one that my father had sung to her in 1939 called My Persian Rosebud. There were already no dry eyes left when Jenny sang in her beautiful alto voice, pleading that we all spend just one more Christmas together. "This is the time for hoping and dreaming, wishing and scheming," she sang. "But what if all the wishes were through and I had to choose one wish, just one wish for you?"

I'd wish for One More Merry Christmas,

A fond forever with my friends,
And if I get my wish this Christmas
I'd wish it never ends!

We didn't know if this would ever happen again. None of us were really home, but then again, all of us were. I think that many an Anglo-Indian can say that they are always home wherever they are.

I heard an American Indian elder, of the indigenous peoples of the Americas, tell the story of six generations of her female ancestors. (Americans with ancestry in India are referred to as Indian-Americans. I would therefore be an Anglo-Indian American.) The idea of six generations intrigued me and I researched six generations in my own female line. This is a difficult thing to do, if you are an Anglo-Indian. The male line is always very clear and once you can authenticate the British connection, which is not hard for most of us, the rest is easy through genealogy records or the British Library.

As I've mentioned, my maternal grandfather, Harry Shepherd, was born in Trowbridge, England. My maternal grandmother, Florence Grace Shepherd nee Lilywhite, was born in India. Her mother, Florence Lillian Lilywhite nee Clapham was also born in India, as was her mother, Jane Debeux Clapham. Anglo-Indians are connected all over the world. Our flag, whatever it might be, is always aloft and the sun never sets on it.

I enacted the stories of these six generations. Generation One was Jane Debeaux, we don't know much about her but my newfound cousin, Ruth, had a picture of her sister. I wore an outfit from the time and talked about her, based on as much information as I could find. Generation Two was my great grandmother Florence Lillian, called Lily but also Lulu, according to my mum. Her father, a side note that has special implications of pleasure for me, also called her Joy. She was the one who was abandoned by her husband and lost her precious son to him. She had to work which was unheard of in those days. She loved to read the classics and spent her Sundays reading. Generation Three was Florence Grace, my grandmother. Unfortunately, she was a chain smoker—very avant-garde in those days—who died of cancer in England. She used to have table-rapping tea parties and produced nine children, of which my mother was the second.

Parts of a letter from my great grandmother to my mother in 1944.

Generation Four was my mother. It was especially good for her grandchildren to hear her tell her own life story. A devout Christian, she gave credit to the Lord Jesus for all the triumphs and victories in her life. She gave her testimony and passed out a little booklet that she had made. She told us how she started her own business in Australia after the age of fifty and made a huge success of it, selling handmade lace from India on the party plan. At one stage, before she retired and sold the business to my sister, Margo, she had a hundred women giving the parties and selling lace for her all over Australia. My sister then created The Lace Place and incorporated lace crafts into her products.

My mother, Isabel, spends some of her time completing a dream she and my dad shared, which was to fund a Christian retreat center in India. Elim in Whitefield, near Bangalore, is the fulfillment of this dream. She raises funds to support many indigenous missionaries in India. When the great tsunami hit, she raised funds to rebuild a church on the Andaman Islands. She has pursued these interests during most of her life.

Then it came to me to stand up for Generation Five. I am a faculty member at a community college in the San Francisco Bay Area in California. I love California, but it is a rare thing for me to meet another Anglo-Indian. Fortunately, I have met many now through the charity picnics and balls we carry out each year to raise funds for Anglo-Indians in India as the West Coast Anglo-Indian group affiliated with CTR. Thanks to the ubiquitous Indian restaurants in Silicon Valley, I can enjoy a South Indian dosai every week, if I want. I cook my favorites dishes: ground meat keema, dal mash, chicken curry, masala fish fry or chili omelets. For Generation Six, my daughter, Sheila wrote a lovely poem that pulled it all together. Sheila brought all her cousins up to the front.

We were not colonists nor were we the colonized; we were simply the offspring of both the colonists and the colonized in India. Six generations of my female ancestors were born in India. We could go way back further than that. We cheated a bit because we wanted to follow the female line. We could have gone back to the first male, George Honey, who came to India two hundred years ago on the ship Minerva. George was an Acting Quartermaster Sergeant, later known as "The Man of Kent." He arrived in 1827 from Maidenstone, Kent, 5 ft 5¼ inches tall, 24 years old, with a long visage, brown hair and grey eyes. He came to India and married Charlotte Young, an Indo-

European who lived in India. Perhaps some Portuguese, perhaps more Indian—we don't really know her genetic makeup and now, so far into the future, it does not matter. When my daughters were in elementary school in California, they were asked to fill out forms stating their race. This is a ridiculous question to ask a child unless they've been carefully schooled by their parents to recognize one race from the other. They looked to one side at their Japanese friend and to the other at an African American, then they all checked Hawaiian. That seemed like a good race to be.

Alas, our imaginary flags came down and we dispersed to the different countries where we now lived in our new homes, the homes of our choosing—or, perhaps, as in my case, the homes that chose us. When Dad died in Brisbane, Australia I thought "Poor Dad, he's buried so far from home" and my sister said, "No, he loved the Broncos and they practice not far from here, so he'll feel at home." Home is always just where you are—Australia, America, Ireland, Canada, New Zealand, England, or India even Kuwait or Dubai— wherever Anglo-Indians are. Let them raise the flag!

First published by CTR. Chase, Joy "*Five Flags*" in *The Way We Are; an Anglo-Indian Mosaic*. Lumb, Lionel and Deborah Van Veldhuisen, editors. CTR Inc. Publishing, New Jersey, USA. 2008. P 186-192.

23

FULL CIRCLE: AN ANGLO-INDIAN REUNION

W hen I heard that the Eleventh World Anglo-Indian Reunion would be held in Madras / Chennai in 2019, I decided I had to attend. It was organized and orchestrated by Harry McClure, editor and publisher of Anglos in the Wind and many other publications. The All-India Anglo-Indian Association has branches all over India, in small towns and large, wherever Anglo-Indians live and congregate. The Federation of Anglo-Indian Associations in India comprises of the Anglo-Indian organizations in India. They hold their Annual General Meeting (AGM) at the world Anglo-Indian reunion, whenever it takes place. The theme of this reunion was Camaraderie on the Coromandel Coast, and it met this goal for most attendees. These reunions have been organized all over the world every three years for the last thirty years, a testament to the global connectedness of Anglo-Indians. This particular reunion, being both in my hometown and in my community, was one I did not want to miss. Perhaps I believed that there would be a recognition of the deep connection we all have, but it was probably overblown in my mind. Anglo-Indians just want to be together and that is the most meaningful.

I was able to forge deeper connections with my younger cousins,

Tim, Sharon, Heather, and their families. They are all related to me on my dad's side, the Chase side.

I skipped the official tour of Madras, spending my time instead in a gold shop and viewing piles of silk saris and pashminas in a shop with a live display of a skilled worker weaving a sari. I missed seeing my old college, Queen Mary's, my school Doveton-Corrie's, and places of worship such as Christ Church and the Vepery Gospel Hall. St. George's Cathedral, built in 1815, stands majestically on Cathedral Road and I did a drive by. Although not members of this cathedral, my family attended many events there when we lived in Madras. I had a peek of this cathedral and its grounds while at the reunion. The tour was not designed to visit all the places that were meaningful to me, of course. These were personal memories from my own childhood and youth. I wished to see the blue ocean with its third largest world-class beach. However, when I went to the MGM Resort for one of the dances, I felt the breeze, but the beach and the ocean itself were hidden in the dark. It took almost three hours to reach this resort, even though we left early to avoid the traffic. Our return trip took less than an hour. Other places I wish I had been able to visit were the State Bank of India, originally the Bank of Madras, on First Line Beach Road, where my dad had worked as the Chief Accountant; the General Hospital with its "No Honking" zone in front; Parry's Corner, with a thousand people milling around; Memorial Hall, a place of many events and classes in my youth; the clock tower near Wilfred Pereira's chemist and gift shop; and the Marina. After all the years and the immense growth of the city, I did not know where I was most of the time, until someone pointed out the corner, the building, the original street names. Then I felt grounded and home.

Thomas Wolfe wrote the novel *You Can't Go Home Again*, and maybe he was right. You can go back to that memory you have of home, but home is just not home anymore. When you leave, and you've been away a long time, people change, die, or move away. Things change. Bridges are built. Roads are renamed and skyways created. People move from one part of the city to another, or to another city. Attitudes change. Government and politics change. Yes, you cannot go home again. But when you do, you might find that certain things remain as they were—timeless and changeless. Some people I knew sixty years ago are still there, and friendships have not faded with distance or time. Those long-ago childhood friends are now active, contributing citizens working hard on the behalf of their community and their families day in and day out. While you are away, your home evolves. New leaders emerge and new concepts are adopted.

I did attend this 11th Anglo-Indian Reunion in Chennai in 2019. Chennai used to be called Madras, but was always known as Chennai in Tamil, the language of the eponymous state, but many locals still call it Madras. They ignore the signs and call everything by the names from fifty or one hundred years ago, some names go even longer back in time. Mount Road, where my father started his first job at the age of eighteen at the Imperial Bank of India, and where the current State Bank of India is extant, is still known as Mount Road even though it was renamed Anna Salai decades ago. This road leads straight to St. Thomas' Mount. It also leads to the Grand Trunk Road, which can take you all the way to Calcutta. It is over 400 years old, going back to its origins as a cart track.

It felt like I had come full circle. Many Anglo-Indians returned to India for this reunion from all over the world—Canada, Australia, New Zealand, England, and the United States. They had all changed and taken on some of the characteristics and accents of their adopted countries. Anglo-Indians who had remained in India had adapted to the new independent environment. They too had to survive, find jobs, negotiate rents or mortgages, and raise their children.

It felt really special to be part of my own large and diverse community. Some of the returning Anglo-Indians tended to stay with their country or family groups. Many others just enjoyed the luxury of shopping or indulging in longed-for sweets and curries, which cannot quite be reproduced exactly abroad. Even the coffee and the tea tasted special, more earthy there. Those who were from Madras spent time seeking out old homes, haunts, or schools of their childhoods. While I enjoyed the shopping and foods, I also wanted to make new friends, spend time with friends from back in America and put personalities to the faces I knew from social media. There was not sufficient time for all of this. I had sought out schools and homes years before when my dear cousin, Dorothea was still with us. I did attend one school reunion in a hotel and was overjoyed to find at least one classmate from my kindergarten year, Celia. It was wonderful to reconnect with her, but it was sad to discover a big divide between the older and younger generations. I would have more enjoyed being with both groups, together, with more activities for connection and face-to-face discussions.

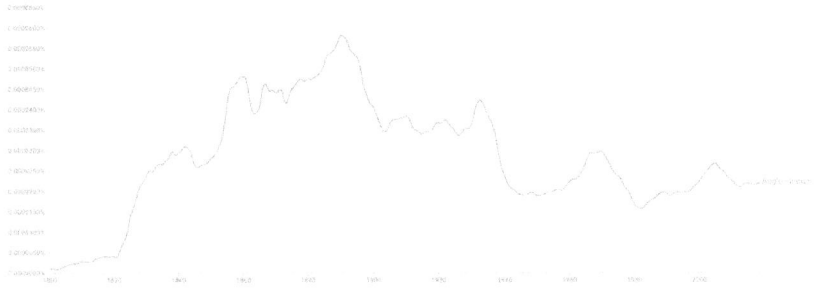

An Ngram of the use of the word "Anglo-Indian" in Google Books 1800-2019

Although I keenly missed my cousin Dorothea, I was delighted to get to know her children who had grown up confident and popular with homes and families of their own. This too felt like completing a circle for me. I loved Kilpauk where I stayed with Timmy and Pinky, it felt like the old Madras of my memories with big trees filled with green parrots and wide roads. In other areas that should have been familiar, I felt lost and disoriented. We went to several colleges for meetings. The reunion was run like a conference, but without nametags or program sheets that would have fostered integration and networking. Queen Mary's college, my alma mater, had become a government-run college and it was not on the list.

The Scott's Kirk in Madras showing the round sanctuary

Not included in the visits and tours was one of the oldest and largest churches in Asia, St. Andrews Church, known as the Scott's Kirk. It has a tall steeple, 112 feet tall which is 166 feet above the ground, built uniquely in the round. It was designed and built by Major Thomas de Havilland (Times of India TOI Apr. 5, 2018). It was completed in 1821 with a round dome painted in blue lapis lazuli with gold stars. I attended this church as a college student when I hosteled at the YWCA down the street. Instead, the Anglo-Indian conference met at Santhome Cathedral Basilica in Mylapore which was originally built by the Portuguese in 1523 and rebuilt in 1896. A side trip was made to the Roman Catholic Marian shrine at Velankanni. I remember going with my dad to St. Thomas Church in Mylapore that had a beautiful organ in it, with strings that stretched across the ceiling. Known as St. Thomas-by-the-sea it was built in 1842 and is now known as St. Thomas English Church in Santhome and belongs to the Church of South India. Santhome is the area where the apostle St. Thomas was martyred and buried and is remembered.

I went to Guindy, which had seemed very far away as a child growing up in Madras. Although it still took over an hour to reach in today's traffic, it is a lot closer to the center as the city has grown to its outer limits. Traffic has multiplied many times over, leaving absolutely no space for the trams that ran up and down Poonamalee High Road until the mid-1940s. I remember riding the trams and listening to their clanging early in the mornings. For a few annas, they ran on the rails and rang their bells from early morning to late at night. The square half-anna piece was still in use then and was a typical fare. The 1940s, right after the war, were nevertheless a lot quieter than the city is today. Maybe the bold new Chennai Metro will be more adapted to the city's current needs, akin to the old electric trains.

My dad used to say that the shape of India looked like a nose, near Chennai, smelling the fragrant spices grown and used there. The ancient and varied indigenous spices of Tamilnadu delight the senses in a deep and primal way. I enjoyed the dosais, idlis, sambar, sapads and pickles and other typical south Indian vegetarian dishes. Although I can get them quite easily here in Silicon Valley, there in Madras, they had more depth and flavor than anything outside of Madras. In the railway junctions, like Basin Bridge and Katpadi, Anglo-Indian life used to revolve around the churches, the schools, and the clubs.

My father was born in Katpadi and I still long to visit that now bustling, throbbing city on the railway gauge line between Chennai and Tirupati, just north of Vellore. I want to see that Railway Station Junction where three generations of my father's family, the Chases, worked and lived. Dr. Ida Scudder, like my great aunt Dr. Esther Chase, realized the great need for female medical care and tended to that need. My great aunt Esther attended medical college in London and returned to work in the Zenana mission in Madras. She lived and ran a clinic at what is now the YWCA on Poonamalee High Road, with a lake and fine grounds around it. Dr. Ida, started the Christian Medical College and Hospital in Vellore.

I really wanted to go to Katpadi and experience the pulsating noises of the Southern Railway trains and the Indian Railway engines; the Katpadi station with its twin-engine auto-rickshaw tuk tuks, its huge promotional movie ads, honking taxis and big yellow station signs in three languages—Tamil, Hindi, and English—declaring it the Katpadi Junction in each script. The trains often run late now, without the disciplined Anglo-Indian drivers. Loud announcements on the PA system add to the cacophony of the station. We used to recreate the station sounds as a game, with various groups taking up typical railway calls and sounds—kapi (coffee), channa (fried split peas), chicku (nut sweets), patani (peanuts)—and someone would always choose to be the whistle. It was raucous fun.

At this World Reunion I was very satisfied to find the Anglo-Indian community, both from outside India and those based in India, to be healthy and strong. I wanted more gatherings, which would have created exchanges of ideas, like focus groups. Some scholars have organized themselves to carry the torch. The majority of these researchers seem not to have a direct Anglo-Indian experience but come to their research and their curiosity obliquely by marriage or through one-sided ancestry. It feels a bit like we are being studied and observed like animals in a zoo, but I say, bully for them because someone is taking an interest in a community that is changing so dynamically as time goes on. We need all the insight we can get.

An existential question often posed by those within and outside the Anglo-Indian community is whether the community is dying, and will it soon be extinct through the dilution of cultural values and inter-marriage? Here in India, there are signs that this community is changed but very much alive. I predict they will persevere, however morphed they may become, and will retain some structures, faith, friendship, and traditions to sustain the community long into the future.

I have come full circle in other ways. Although I have been back to India many times and to Madras several times, this time felt very connecting and complete. Mount Road is still very much there. The Protestant churches are filled, and the Roman Catholic churches are robust. I felt the comfort of hearing, and sometimes understanding, the mellifluous Tamil language. The delightful vegetarian restaurants have not changed, although they are now swarmed by motorbikes and Google Eats couriers delivering meals wrapped in banana leaves to every corner of the city.

The silver thread that runs through all Anglo-Indians is still evident, especially when we meet. It is one of a certain culture, a bond, a tie and the spirit of the Raj and those intrepid entrepreneurs and pioneers who instilled in us a desire for exploration and a thirst for adventure. Against all odds, the passion for living is good and well for Anglo-Indians all over the world, such that those who a have a slight awareness of the community through one parent, a grandparent or even a more distant ancestor want to study us, trace their roots, and claim the Anglo-Indian community as their own. Will the Anglo-Indian community die out or disappear? I don't think so, not any time soon. They continue to rise like the phoenix from the embers and ashes of our centuries-old community.

I don't know if I will ever return to Madras, but it will always, always remain deep in my heart and my Anglo-Indian roots will shine in me forever.

As Br. Chan Phap Dung, a monk at Plum Village Buddhist Monastery founded by Zen Master Thich Nhat Han, in southern France says:

> The message is to remember we don't come from nowhere. We have roots. We have ancestors. We are part of a lineage or stream.

PART FIVE
END NOTES

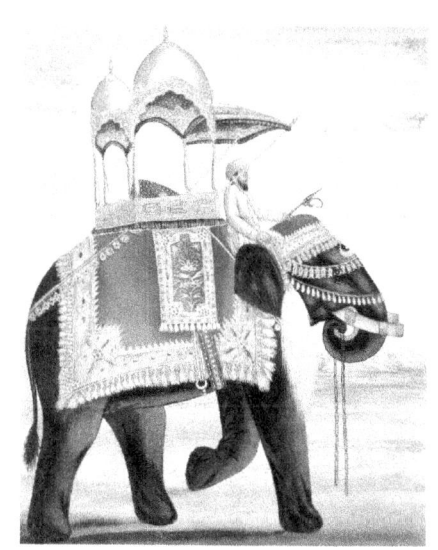

24

A COLLECTION OF RECIPIES

This section of a few selected recipes has been chosen for the love I have of these dishes. Choosing two or three to make for a meal jogs my olfactory senses and softens my eyes bringing to my heart the sensual memories of dishes prepared in India, many years ago. I hope you enjoy them and have no trouble procuring the ingredients and converting to British weights and measure or ollucks if you wish. I was able to find the equivalents for Indian weights and measures in an encyclopedia in 1964. Today on 1library.net Venkatesh Parthasarathy in an *Indian Journal of History of Science* (2019), surveys some sources and quotes the second volume of *Oriental Commerce* by William Milburn written in 1813. It was called the Madras Measure: "1 olluck is equal to 11.798 ollucks which make 1 measure or puddy or 93.7528 measure make 1 marcal or 7505 marcal make 1 parah or 3750400 marcal make 1 garce or 300,00". Later they measured against grams. First the weight of the measure, an olluck, then the equivalent for a flat or heaped measure. By 1935 they defined further that one olluck had an internal diameter of 2 1/2" x 3 1/8" deep. The weight of one olluck measure minus the weight of the measure itself was 224 grams. This is equivalent to 7.9 ounces or 1 cup. There you have it.

Baked Custard

We loved my mum's baked custard and she made it often over the years so that her children and grandchildren love it, too. As she came into her 90s and stopped cooking, my sister Margo started making it for her. Naturally, I asked them both of for their recipes and my daughter also requested it. An emailed recipe to my daughter Natala from my mum Isabel in 2002 states 1 ½ pints of full cream milk with 5 eggs. This recipe was consistent with her email to me in 2006. Margo's "Mum's Baked Custard" recipe 2020 says to use 1 quart of full cream milk with 4 eggs but another says to use 1 pint (USA) full cream milk and only 3 eggs. Even better, an undated recipe from my sister says to use only 2 eggs but add a tin of condensed milk. The sugar and vanilla remained constant, except that my mother suggested 2 scoops of sugar with no explanation. I had to create an aggregate. The secret seems to be leaving the custard in the oven until it is cool, 3-5 hours or overnight.

Time: 45 minutes plus time to cool
Serves: 4

Ingredients:

>   4 eggs
>   1 tsp vanilla
>   ½ cup castor sugar (or regular white sugar)
>   1-quart full cream milk, warmed
>   ½ tsp cinnamon sugar, optional

Method:
Heat oven to 350F or 180C. Beat the eggs, add the sugar and vanilla essence until frothy. Add warmed milk slowly. Pour into baking dish and sprinkle cinnamon sugar on top, if preferred. Bake for 40-45 minutes. Switch off the oven and leave custard to cool in the oven before refrigerating.

Beef Vindaloo

My mother Isabel gave me this recipe over the phone in the 1980s because I was asked to make an Indian meal for my church. I made the recipe in three batches and, with the help of many church volunteers, made enough for 75 people. I used ready-made curry pastes and canned tomatoes to save on labor and time. The dinner was appreciated. This dish is great made with pork, too. I have reduced the recipe for 6 people. Sometimes the mixes are more complex than the ingredients we can procure easily in the west and often the ingredients are fresher than stale curry powders that are not fresh ground.

Time: 30 minutes preparation time plus 2 hours cooking time. Less for smaller quantities
Serves: 25 or 6

Ingredients:

For 25 servings:
30 tbs Vindaloo paste
15 onions, chopped
25 lbs. beef rump roast, cut in 1-inch cubes
5 tsp salt
60 oz tomato puree
10 potatoes
10 tbs vinegar
10 tsp chili powder
2 ½ cups oil
1 cup water

For 6 servings
2 tbs Vindaloo paste*
2 onions, medium-sized, chopped
2 lb. beef or pork, cut up
1 tsp salt
5 tomatoes

2 potatoes, medium-sized
2 tbs vinegar
1 tbs chili powder (Kashmiri mirch)
6 tbs oil
½ cup water (or, as needed)

* Homemade vindaloo paste. Servings: 1 cup (save to use later)
Ingredients: 5 tbs Kashmiri chili powder, 2 tbs paprika, ½ tsp
turmeric, ¼ tsp ground cumin, 2 tbs oil, ¼ tsp salt, ¼ tsp ground
coriander, 1 tsp brown sugar, 4 tsp tamarind water or vinegar, 6 tbs
garlic ginger paste. Method: puree in processor or blender. Add
splashes of water, if needed. (I use Patak's Vindaloo paste as it is good
and saves time.)

Method:
Puree the tomatoes and half the chopped onions. Peel and cut up
potatoes. Heat oil on top of stove. Add the other half of the chopped
onions. When the onion is glazed brown, add the Vindaloo Paste and
chili powder. Sauté, stirring constantly for 1-2 mins.

Add ½ cup water and continue sautéing, stirring constantly, for 2-3
minutes more. Add the beef or pork. Mix in well.

Add salt. Sauté for 20 mins, stirring often to make sure the spices and
onions do not burn. The juice from the meat will come out now. Add
the tomato and onion puree.

Mix everything well in pan, partially cover pan and cook for a total of
two hours till the meat is tender and oil separated. Smaller quantities
of meat will take less time. Check and mix often.

Add the cut-up potatoes while the sauce is still simmering. Let them
cook in sauce for 20 minutes. Take out the potatoes and reserve if they
are done but leave in to cook if needed. Simmer for another 45
minutes.

Add the vinegar and mix in well. Put stove on low and simmer the rest of the time, about 30 mins (if needed). Keep partially covered but stir occasionally. Add in a little bit of water to keep from burning. Add in the reserved potatoes. The vindaloo should be a rich red color now. Serve hot with cooked white rice.

Country Captain (chicken)

Country Captain has early origins, probably around the 16th century. It is said that a cook created it as an attempt to blend European and Indian epicurean delights. Perhaps the word captain is a misnamed capon from the French. We know that this dish has circled the globe ending up as a Southern specialty in Charleston and Savannah, port cities of Georgia in America. It is elevated to General Chicken in Chinese restaurants and it was included in the *Joy of Cooking* by Irma S. Rombauer going back to 1931. It is the most iconic of Anglo-Indian dishes.

Time: 30 minutes
Serves: 6

Ingredients:

1 lb. chicken parts (preferably bone-in thighs)
3 large onions, sliced finely
3 tbs coconut oil (or as preferred)
1 tsp turmeric
1 tsp mild chili powder
1 tsp ground black peppercorns
3-4 dried red chilis, deseeded
5 garlic pods, crushed
2 tbs ginger, grated
2 pieces of cinnamon
3-5 cloves
6-8 whole black peppercorns
1 cup chicken stock or water

¼ cup currents
¼ cup sliced almonds
Juice of half a lemon
Salt to taste

Method:
Heat the oil and brown the chicken parts and set aside. Add the sliced onions, garlic and ginger and sauté until golden. Remove one third of cooked onions and set aside. Add the turmeric, chili powder, peppercorns, cinnamon, and cloves. Add a little chicken stock or water and sauté. Add the browned chicken, add rest of chicken stock and cover, and cook until done (about 20 minutes). Add lemon juice and salt. In separate pan, continue to sauté the onion garlic ginger mixture that was set aside. Allow to brown darker and add the slit and deseeded dried red chilis, currants and almond slices. Serve the chicken with the additional fried onions, currents, almond slices, and red chili on top of the chicken to make a festive-looking dish. Serve with cooked hot white rice.

The author

Dal Mash (using Mung Dal)

My aunt Daphne had given me her recipe for Dal Mash, and it was years later that I was advised to eat mung dal every day for my health. Mung dal is especially good for gut health. My mung dal recipe follows, combined with the dal mash recipe. Note: be careful with the turmeric as it tends to stain.

Time: 30-40 minutes
Serves: 6 or 1 for 6 days

Ingredients:

   1 cup organic mung dal (other dal can be used instead)
   1 tsp black mustard seeds
   1 tsp cumin seeds
   1 tsp ground turmeric
   6 cups water
   3 tbs oil
   Salt
   Curry leaves (optional)

Method:
Soak the dal for several hours or overnight. Drain and set aside. Heat the oil in a large pan. These pans are called dekshis in India, but my adult children don't remember or use the word. Add the black mustard and cumin seeds and let them simmer until the mustard starts popping and jumping all over your stove top. Add the dal carefully, the oil will be hot. Add the turmeric and salt and mix well. Add the water, mix and allow to simmer on low heat until the dal is soft and can be mashed smooth. Add the curry leaves and allow to cool. Other ingredients like coconut milk, tomatoes, lemon or tamarind juice and cilantro can be added but for health reasons and a pure diet, I keep this dish very simple. Serve with simple steamed white rice or with additional dishes.

Fish and Mango Curry

I remember fish curry with green mangoes in Madras when I was growing up. I loved the tangy taste of the mangoes and the bite of green chilies straight off our chili plant. Bridget White's recipe from her book *A Collection of Simple Anglo-Indian Recipes* is excellent. Her authentic Anglo-Indian recipes are available on her blog http://anglo-indianrecipes.blogspot.com/ and her books on Amazon or via PayPal. I am indebted to Bridget for much of this recipe.

Time: 45 minutes
Serves: 4

Ingredients:

1 lb. or ½ kg any firm fish cut into medium pieces.
I used rock cod as it was the only fish that my grocery delivery had during the pandemic. It was good but I like halibut better.
1 tsp ginger paste
1 tsp garlic paste, or fresh garlic smashed
1 green chili
2 tbs cilantro leaves or to taste
½ tsp cumin
1 tsp chili powder
¼ tsp turmeric powder
½ tsp coriander powder
Above 4 ingredients can be substituted by 2 tsp curry powder or paste.
¼ tsp salt or, to taste
2 tbs oil
1 firm mango (green, if available)
1 onion
½ cup unsweetened coconut milk

Bridget White Kumar with me in Madras, 2019

Method:
Cook the mango pieces with the chopped green chili and a pinch of turmeric in a little water till soft. Keep aside. Heat oil in pan and sauté the onions till golden brown. Add the turmeric powder, chili powder, ginger and garlic, cumin powder, coriander powder, coconut paste and salt and mix well. Keep sauteing on low heat till the oil separates and comes to the top. Add the fish and cooked mango pieces and a little more water, if required, and cook for 7-8 minutes till the fish is done. Garnish with the chopped cilantro leaves. Serve hot with steamed white rice.

Fougarth (made with cabbage)

Fougarths are a nutrient-dense side-dish that often accompanies an afternoon meal of Curry & Rice. Make it with any leafy vegetable you prefer. I like making this dish with rainbow chard or any available chard. My mother Isabel always liked to make it with cabbage. Her grandkids loved it and asked her for the recipe. This is the recipe that she emailed to my daughter, Natala in 2002.

Time: 10 minutes
Serves: 4-6

Ingredients:

>   3 tbs oil
>   ½ large cabbage
>   ½ tsp black mustard seed
>   1 large onion
>   ½ tsp turmeric powder
>   Fresh green [coriander] cilantro leaves
>   ¼ tsp salt
>   2 tbs grated fresh coconut, or unsweetened grated dried
>   coconut (optional)

Method:
Shred the cabbage finely. Fry (sauté) in oil the half a teaspoon of black mustard seed, when it pops add one large onion that has been cut up small till it turns transparent. Add cabbage, salt, a little turmeric, and some chopped coriander leaf. Don't over fry. It should be taken off the fire before the water comes out of the cabbage. Cook about two minutes. [Isabel Chase email to Natala Menezes January 11, 2002]

Kedgeree (Dal and Rice)

The movie *A Passage to India* came out in 1984 and won many awards. I had an article published on March 20, 1985, in the San Jose Mercury News[paper] in Section E. I suggested an Indian party as an accompaniment to watching the movie. It was titled "Rich Flavor of the Raj; Anglo-Indian culture is more than a movie" and included this recipe. The movie was based on a novel by the same name written by E.M. Forster in 1924. It deals with the issues of racism and colonialism ahead of current discussions. Although kedgeree is a traditional vegetarian Indian dish dating back to the 1300s, it was adopted by the British and includes smoked salmon or haddock and even eggs.

Time: 35 minutes
Serves 6

Ingredients:

1 onion
3 tbs oil
1/2 tsp cumin seeds
1 tsp turmeric
2 cups white rice
1 cup soaked yellow dal (split peas)
6 cups water
salt to taste

Method:
Slice onion finely. Heat oil in pan on medium heat. Add onion and sauté till lightly browned. Add cumin and turmeric and sauté an additional 1-2 minutes. Add rice and mix well. Wash and add split peas, water, and salt. Mix, cover firmly and cook on low/medium heat for 30 minutes. Remove from heat and leave covered for 5 minutes. Mix gently with a fork and serve hot. Serve with salmon.

Isabel's Pilau (Prawn Vermicelli Pilau)

My mother Isabel used to make this dish to perfection. I've never been able to match hers. Try to get the finest vermicelli you can. This makes it a light and delicious pilau. My siblings and I all love this dish.

Time: 15 minutes cooking time
Serves: 4

Ingredients:

1 pkt egg noodles (these must be broken up)
1 large onion, cut up small
3 Tbs oil
1 Tbs green masala* (or make your own)
1 cup plain yogurt
1 lb. shelled, cleaned prawns

2 carrots, cut up into small squares
1 cup fresh cooked or frozen peas
3 eggs
Salt to taste
1 bunch cilantro (green coriander)

Method:
After breaking up the egg noodles into small pieces, put in a wok or frying pan and dry fry with no oil. Keep turning but don't allow to brown. Next place in a pan of boiling water and cook until el dente according to the package directions. Strain and set aside.

Add oil to a pan and sauté the chopped onion until translucent. Add one heaped Tbs of green masala paste and sauté for a couple of minutes. Add a little water to keep from burning. * Make your own green masala if it is unavailable in your area. Combine 1 or two bunches of green coriander (cilantro) with 2 green chilies. A pinch each of pepper, cloves, cinnamon, cumin seeds, ginger, garlic, and turmeric. Add some salt and blend with a squeeze of lemon juice or ¼ cup vinegar.

Add a small carton of plain yogurt. Cook for a short while. There should not be too much liquid. If it seems to have too much liquid cook longer before adding prawns. Then add the prawns. Now cook only for about a minute because the longer you cook will make the prawns tough.

Cook the carrots and peas separately in a steamer or boiling water. Strain and set aside.

Beat the eggs and make a plain flat omelet and cut into one-inch pieces. Set aside.

Now, mix the cooked carrots, peas, omelet in the prawn mixture. Add the noodles and salt. Mix well for about a minute. Add chopped cilantro. All done, tastes delicious!

Podalong Kai (Stuffed Snake Coy Curry aka stuffed zucchini)

This was always my birthday request because once a year, my mother allowed me to choose the menu for the day. The so-called snake coys are gourds that grows on a tree and when they grow really long, they looked like snakes. We used the smaller ones, more the size of large home-grown zucchini. When it is difficult to find podalang kai, I substitute with zucchini.

Time: 30 minutes
Serves: 4

Ingredients:

    1 lb. ground beef or chicken
    1 medium sized snake gourd or 4 medium zucchinis
    2 medium onions
    1 green chili, chopped
    3 large tomatoes, pureed or ½ 12 oz can pureed tomatoes
    1/2 cup coconut milk, canned
    1 tsp ginger paste or chopped fresh ginger
    1 tsp garlic paste or chopped fresh garlic pods
    2 tsp chili powder
    2 tsp coriander powder
    1 tsp turmeric powder
    Salt to taste
    3 Tbs oil
    1 bunch of cilantros (green coriander), chopped

Method:
Cut the zucchinis into 2-inch chunks and clean out the seeds and inner sections. Set aside.

Mix half of the masala powders (coriander, chili, turmeric and salt) with the ground meat and let sit to blend.
Chop the onions small. Heat the oil in a pan and sauté the onions

until translucent. Add the green chili, garlic, and ginger. Sauté a few minutes longer. Add the other half of the masala powders and continue to sauté. Add the coconut milk and the pureed tomatoes and cook until married. Then add two cups of water and bring to a boil and cook down to a sauce.

Stuff the zucchinis with the ground meat which has blended well with the spices. Push the meat down into the zucchinis to make them stay in the rounds. Drop them gently into the curry sauce and cook on low heat till the gravy is thick and the meat cooked. Add the chopped cilantro. Serve hot.

Grandma Adelaide's Fish Fry

My grandmother, my dad's mother: Adelaide Blanche Chase Raikes, used to make this dish. My dad loved it and when he and my mother emigrated to Australia, he used to make it often. I asked him how he learned to make this dish and he said that he learned how his mother made it when he was a teenager helping his mother to cook. He was her sous-chef cutting up, prepping and observing.

Time: 30 minutes
Serves 4.

Ingredients:

> 1 tbs balsamic vinegar (or whatever vinegar you have)
> 1 tsp red chili powder
> 1 tsp turmeric powder
> 1 tsp coriander powder
> (Above 3 ingredients can be substituted by one tbs vindaloo paste)
> 4 tbs light vegetable oil
> 1 lb. white fish, halibut preferred
> 1 large onion
> salt

Method:

In a bowl, mix the powders with the vinegar until blended. Spread the paste with salt onto the sides of the fish, evenly and lightly. Sauté in the 3 tbs oil for 5 minutes or less on one side and turn over only once and sauté on second side until done, but not overdone. Check the fish often and make sure the paste is not raw.

Slice the onion thinly. In another pan, heat 1 tbs oil and sauté the onion slices until brown and pour over the fish.

Serve with a side of tomatoes and green chilies with plain yogurt and hot white rice.

Love Cake

My mother knew the Poulier sisters at her church in Sri Lanka and their cooking inspired her. They influenced, to a much greater extent, the famed cookbook author, Charmain Solomon. Charmain's memories are beautifully rendered in her book *Love and a Wooden Spoon* (1984, 1985). This recipe, however, came from my mother's good friend Valerie Anthonisz Collette, who she also knew from her church in Colombo, Ceylon. I have adapted it to the modern American kitchen. It has Dutch, Portuguese and Old-World influences that make it a rich and hearty dessert.

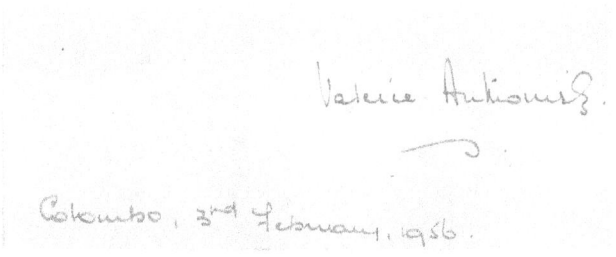

Valerie signed my autograph book in 1956

Time: one hour, once all ingredients are sourced, prepped, and assembled

Serves: 6

Ingredients:

8 oz butter
1 lb. (16 oz) white sugar—use superfine caster sugar if available
8 oz semolina (durum wheat), lighted toasted
8 eggs
8 oz roasted unsalted cashew nuts, minced small
8 oz candied fruit—if unavailable use dried fruits
3 oz honey
1 tsp vanilla essence, add 1 tsp rose water, if available
Zest of 1 lemon or lime
½ tsp each—ground cinnamon, cloves, and nutmeg
4 oz plain flour

Method:
Beat softened butter and sugar until light and creamy. Add semolina that has been toasted to a caramel color in a dry pan and cooled. Add 5 eggs and 3 yolks one at a time. Add minced cashew nuts. Mince the dried or candied fruit small. (If the dried fruit is too hard, soak in a couple of tbs brandy or plain water. Dry and coat thinly with flour to keep the fruit from drifting to the bottom of the cake while being baked.) Add fruit to batter and add honey, zest, essences, and spices and mix well. Beat the remaining 3 egg whites well and fold in. Sprinkle rest of flour and mix lightly with a wooden spoon. Pour into square pan and sprinkle top with 1 tbs sugar. Bake for 45 minutes at 350F. Do not let it get too dry. Remove from oven while center is still soft and allow to cool.

Mulligatawny Soup

My mother Isabel loved to make this soup, especially for guests. It takes three days, but it is well worth it. It is an Anglo-Indian standard.

Time: as needed. 2 hours to 3 days.
Serves 4 - 6

Ingredients:

2 tbs ghee or oil
1 onion
6 curry leaves
½ tsp cumin powder
½ tsp ginger and garlic
1/8 tsp peppercorns, ground
¼ tsp chili powder
¼ tsp salt, or to taste
¼ tsp coriander powder
½ cup of water and 1 cup later
1 breast of chicken with bone (lamb breast is best)
4 cups chicken stock
½ cup coconut milk (fresh or canned)
Bunch of fresh coriander (cilantro) leaves

Method:
Heat the ghee or oil in a large pan. Chop the onion and sauté till translucent. Add spices and sauté with ¼ cup water to keep from burning. Add chicken breast and coat with spice mixture then add chicken stock and simmer for an hour. (If using lamb breast, cool in the fridge overnight and remove oil from top before continuing.)

On the second hour (or second day) remove the chicken breast or lamb breast and mix in the coconut milk. Add some water, if needed. Heat, cooking till well married.

Serve with the chicken shredded (or lamb breast bones removed). Discard the bones. Add some cooked white rice in the bowls and fresh coriander leaves on top as a garnish. Serve hot as an appetizer or main course.

25
A HISTORICAL TIMELINE

It is amazing to me, to think of parallel events that were happening in India and all over the world at the same time. I break it down below and I hope it creates a sense of perspective during India's recent history. What happened in different places? We don't know why they made certain decisions. Did the French really give up America for India? Was it all predestined, fueled by greed, curiosity, and exploration? Or did it just happen? Was it fate? Kismet.

1497-1498 Vasco da Gama discovered an ocean route to India. He became the Viceroy of Portuguese India in 1524.

1599 British East India Company founded

1603 James crowned King of England

1605 Jehangir, son of Akbar the Great crowned Emperor of the Mogul Empire

1625 Charles I crowned King of England

1627 Shah Jehan crowned Emperor of the Mogul Empire

1658 Aurangzeb is crowned over the Mogul Empire

1660 Charles II crowned King of England

1707 Aurangzeb, Emperor of the Mogul Empire, dies.

1747 Battle of Plassey gives Britain control of Bengal

1774 Warren Hastings, Governor-General of India

1776 American Declaration of Independence

1789 French Revolution begins

1799 Tipu Sultan killed at Seringapatam in the Kingdom of Mysore in South India

1804 Napoleon declares himself Emperor of France

1820 George IV crowned King of England

1837 Bahadur Shah II crowned King of Delhi

1837 Queen Victoria crowned Queen of England

1848 Marquis of Dalhousie is Governor-General of India

1857 Indian Mutiny (First War of Independence)

1858 Government of India transferred from East India Company to British Crown

1858 Earl Canning made Viceroy of India

1861 Civil War begins in America

1862 Bahadur Shah II, last Mogul ruler dies

1869 Suez Canal opened

1877 Queen Victoria proclaimed Empress of India

1901 Queen Victoria dies. Edward VII becomes King of England

1910 Edward VII dies. George V crowned King of England.

1911-1912 Revolution in China. Fall of the Qing dynasty End of Imperial China. Establishment of the Republic of China

1914 First World War begins

1922 Gandhi arrested, tried, and imprisoned for sedition and civil disobedience

1930 Gandhi organized the Salt March to protest British Rule in India

1936 King George V dies. Edward VIII ascends to the throne and abdicates. George VI becomes King of England

1939 Second World War starts

1942 Gandhi's Quit India demand

1945 Second World War ends

1947 Viscount Mountbatten of Burma is Viceroy of India

1947 India attained Independence

1948 Apartheid, racial segregation instituted officially in South Africa,

1948 Gandhi assassinated

1948 Muhammad Ali Jinnah, founder of Pakistan, dies

1949 Chinese Communist leader Mao Zedong declared the creation of the People's Republic of China (PRC).

1950 India becomes a Republic

1948-1960 saw a great migration of Anglo-Indians to England, Australia, Canada, and America creating a diaspora of the Anglo-Indian community.

26

VOCABULARY

Akka—although this Tamil word can have several meanings such as mother-in-law, stepmother, adoptive mother but the strongest use is for elder sister, also used as a form of respect.

Almirah—an Anglo-Indian term for a free-standing cupboard to store clothes, probably derived from the eighteenth century

Anna—one Rupee consisted of 16 Annas. In September 1955 the Indian Coinage Act of 1906 was amended to pave the way for the country to decimalize and the anna became obsolete. (The Reserve Bank of India museum.)

Armoire—a wardrobe used in a bedroom to store or hang clothes, usually instead of a built in.

Ashoka—a grand rain forest tree that grows on the Deccan plateau and is known to have spiritual and medicinal qualities

Athma—a Sanskrit word that alludes to the spirit or soul. Mahatma means great soul.

Avant-garde—derived from French, this means experimental, ahead of its time, unorthodox in culture and the arts

Ayah—a word derived from Portuguese for nursemaid and children's maid, used in British India.

Baksheesh—derived from Persian and used in India and the Middle East for a bribe or tip

Bara (burra)—a title used for respect as in an elder brother or chief officer in India

Bas—roughly means enough in Hindi

Bel puri—a complex snack popular in Mumbai

Boo madu—a decorated ox used in Tamilnadu for fortune-telling and entertainment

Broncos—an Australian professional rugby league football club based in Brisbane.

Bundaberg—a brand of excellent rum and ginger beer made in Australia

Bundoo—undefined diminutive for cute as in bundoo boochi meaning "cute little bug"

Butch game—slang used for hopscotch

Casuarina—a tree native to India and Australia, evergreen, tall with pine-like needles

Catty, catapult—a device used to launch a projectile (i.e., a mud ball) some distance

Chai—a Hindi word for tea derived from the Chinese word for tea: cha. Now used universally for masala tea or tea boiled with cardamon and other spices with milk.

Channa—a Hindi word for chickpea. A staple in India.

Chatti—a clay pot

Chhotta haazri —a little breakfast. (Mentioned in Hobson Jobson).

Chokra Chokri—a young staff member (male, female), in their early teens, employed by the house.

Chor—a thief in Hindi, also used by gypsies in Romany which may have derived from India.

Croton—a plant with brightly colored leaves, originating from Indonesia

Crore—ten million or one hundred lakhs especially in rupees but also for other measurements

Cul-culs—or kul-kuls are a sweet made with flour and coconut milk by Anglo-Indians and Goans at Christmas.

Damask—a fabric woven with a pattern on both sides

De la guerre—a French phrase for "that's war" implying that it can't be helped

Deal wood—a soft wood that is easy to saw and relatively inexpensive

Dekshi—generally a pot to cook in but fancy dekshis can be used to serve food dal—dal, dahl is a lentil which is a staple of the Indian diet. There are many varieties.

Dhobi—a washerman

Dho Dhol/Dho Dhol—dohl dohl, is a halwa made with black rice, an Anglo-Indian Christmas tradition

Dosai/dosa—popularly called dosa but dosai in South India it is a savory crepe made from fermented rice and lentils. Masala dosais have a spicy filling of potatoes.

Drawing room—more formal than a living room, it is often reserved for entertaining visitors

Durbar—derived from Persian for a ruler's court coopted by Indian princes and the British

Egg-hopper—a savory crepe with an egg on the top served with sweet coconut milk.

Feng shui—a Chinese system of using energy to inform placement of surroundings in a house

Foogarth/fougarth—perhaps Portuguese in origin—a side-dish of vegetables (often cabbage or green beans) seasoned with coconut and other spices

Garcon de Maison—French for waiter or man/boy employed by the house

Ghat—used in South Asia to mean a range of hills, or hills and valleys even steps leading to a river

Ghoda ghari—a ghari or ghadi is a cart, usually covered, drawn by a ghoda—a horse

Ghurkha—Nepalese soldiers who have units in the Nepalese, Indian and British armies

Godown—a warehouse or storage place used in India and other Asian countries

Goldbees—goldbugs or golden beetles found in North America and at one time, in India, too

Guava cheese—made with fresh guavas in Goa and other parts of India, a chewy halva-like sweet

Hakka—Hakka is a ceremonial Maori dance, call and response, ritual in New Zealand

Halvah/halva—a sesame-based confection common in countries from Turkey to India

Ho gaya—Hindi for finished, completed, or happened

Idli—a traditional breakfast cake in South India made from rice and hulled black gram

Imarti—type of jelebi (see also jelebi) made with urad dal (black gram)

Jai hind—Hindi salutation meaning Victory to India or Long Live India.

Jangiri—similar to Imarti jelebi made from urad dal, often made for holidays in India

Jelebi—a sweet made by frying flour and saffron in round coil-like shapes and then soaked in syrup

Jenever—a juniper-flavored Dutch gin of fine quality

Joie de vivre—French for the joy of life, with exuberance

Jute—derived from the jute plant bark to make natural products such as burlap and twine

Jutka vandi—Tamil for a horse-drawn passenger cart aka ghoda ghari in Hindi

Kai or coi—basically a Tamil word for gourd or vegetable

Kala-azar—a chronic and potentially fatal parasitic tropical disease also called Black Fever

Kapi—phonetic for coffee, usually South Indian filter coffee

Karapodi—silver bellied fish

Keema—literally, minced meet derived from Urdu but often used to describe a curry made with minced lamb or other meat, potatoes, peas and spices

Kela—means banana

Khela—or kayala in Bengali for coal

Khus-khus—or couscous made of durum wheat semolina

Kolis—fishermen who are indigenous to Mumbai

Kumbli boochi—or kambalipoochi literally translated from Tamil as a blanket worm, caterpillar.

Kai varamate—in Tamil this is an idiom meaning literally one's hand has volition and will not allow itself to be extended in generosity

Lakh—one hundred thousand

L'amour—French, for love

Lungi—a type of sarong worn by men in India

Madeira cake—similar to a pound or heavier sponge cake made with (or eaten with) a sweet Madeira (Portuguese) wine

Maharajah/Maharaja—Sanskrit for a great ruler or king

Maidan—derived from Turkish it denotes an open space or field

Maître de—French for master of the house, head waiter, host

Mali—actually a Hindu occupational caste of gardeners in India

Marble cake—alternating layers of colored batter to create a streaked cake that looks like marble

Masala—a mixture of ground spices. Often used to denote any mixture.

Meat-safe—a food-safe with wire meshed sides and doors to keep food fresh before refrigeration

Memsahib—possibly borrowed from Arabic, denotes a woman in a position of authority

Mere as in mere Mumbai—translated from Hindustani as mine, my

Mufti—originating from the Arabic word for scholar, it became British slang for off-duty officers wearing local clothing, maybe they were scholars sometimes

Nom de plume—French for a pen name or pseudonym

O'clock—a contraction of the phrase "of the clock" often referring to an analog clock

Pagodas—the pagoda was a unit of currency, a coin made of gold or half-gold minted by Indian dynasties as well as the British, the French and the Dutch. It was subdivided into 42 fanams. It is also a word for temples that are buildings with many tiered roofs.

Paneer—a fresh unsalted cottage cheese made and used in Indian cuisine

Papadums—thin, crispy side dish made from lentil flour, often dried in the sun

Parottas, Parathas—an Indian bread with a layered texture

Patani—literally translated from Tamil to mean peas, often dried

Peon—possibly derived from Spanish to mean a laborer or worker, often at beck and call

Pepper-water—an Anglo-Indian version of the south Indian rasam served with curry and rice.

Pice—the lowest valued Indian coin before decimalization of the monetary system

Podalong-cai—a wild legume species of vegetable

Pollum—a historic unit of weight used in India equal to approximately one ounce

Pomfret—a kind of flat butterfish found in Indian waters

Punka—a fan used in ancient or rural India made of cloth or palm fronds and moved manually

Purdah—seclusion practiced by Muslim and also Hindu women

Raj Era—or British Raj (raj meaning rule in Sanskrit), the period of time India was officially ruled by the British Crown from 1858 to 1947. It sometimes alludes to a longer span of time when the British were in India and ruled some areas unofficially as the East India Company.

Ragi—a gluten-free whole grain, which is a staple in South India, also known as finger millet

Rajah/raja—a monarch in India whose wife is known as the rani or rana.

Rickshaw—a light, two-wheeled cart. In the past it was pulled by a man but is now motorized

Rickshaw-wallah—the man who pulls the rickshaw, derived from Hindustani meaning man or boy

Rosa (rosie) cuikees (coquese)—a deep fried sweet rose-shaped cookie made by Anglo-Indians at Christmas, called Achu Murukku in Tamil.

Rupee—a unit of currency in India, dating back to ancient days, derived from Sanskrit

Sahib—originally from Arabic or Turkish meaning sir, master, or someone of official status. Pukka sahib is a slang term taken from Hindi to mean a proper gentleman. Sahib is a slang term.

Salaams—gestures of greeting or respect

Sambar—a dish made with vegetables, lentils and spices in South India eaten with dosais or rice. Also, a large deer native to the Indian subcontinent.

Sapad—a traditional Tamil meal often eaten on a banana leaf, prepared according to the ancient Code of Manu—a moral and religious set of laws.

Sarong—a large length of fabric wrapped around the waist. Nowadays often used as swimsuit coverups.

Seer—also known as King Fish, it is found in the Indian ocean

Semai ke rani—Tamil for the Queen of England

Serviette—a French word used in British English for what is called a table napkin in America

Sharkskin—a smooth two-toned woven fabric made from mohair or wool that does not wrinkle easily—it is not made from the skin of a shark.

Siesta—Spanish for a nap, often taken in the afternoon when the tropics are the hottest

Sigiri—a one-pot charcoal stove

Snake coy—a vegetable like zucchini but which grows on a tree and sometimes is so long that it looks like a snake

Stuga—Swedish for a cottage

Sultanas—a kind of raisin made from seedless green grapes

Tiffin-carriers—a many-tiered lunch box, usually made of metal

Topi—a wide-brimmed hat, sometimes made of pith or cork

Tuk tuks/auto-rickshaw—derived from Japanese, basically a 3-wheeled motorized rickshaw

Vindaloo—derived from the Portuguese Carne de Vinha d'alhos, this dish is a popular spicy Goan meat curry

Viss—maybe of Burmese origin, an old unit of measurement before metrics were introduced

Wallah—a Hindi word for man associated with a certain profession for example rickshaw wallah

27
PHOTOGRAPHS AND ILLUSTRATIONS

CREDITS

The photographs in this memoir were mostly taken by me and members of my family, including my daughter Sheila Menezes sheilamenezesphotography.com . Others are from family albums and postcard collections. A few are taken from the Internet under the Creative Commons license, or I was unable to trace the source. Please do not copy or circulate any photos or illustrations from this book. This book is copyrighted.

Elephant painting on paper. 19th Century. British Museum No. 1877,0113,0.65 Public Domain in Britain and the United States.

28

SELECTED BIBLIOGRAPHY

A LIST OF BOOKS CONSULTED AND OF INTEREST

Allen, Charles. *Raj: A Scrapbook of British India, 1877-1947*. Andre Deutsch, 1977. Penguin Books, 1979.

—-. Kipling Sahib; *India and the Making of Rudyard Kipling*. Pegasus Books. 2009.

Ambat, Gladys. *More Grasps to Reach; a Hundred Years of the Madras Y.W.C.A.* Young Women's Christian Association, 1992.

Andrews, Robyn and Merin Simi Raj, editors. *Anglo-Indian Identity: Past and Present, in India and the Diaspora*. Palgrave MacMillan, 2021.

Anthony, Frank. *Britain's Betrayal in India; the Story of the Anglo-Indian Community*. Allied Publishers. 1969. Anglo Indian Heritage series, 2007.

Antrim, Louisa Jane McDonnell. (Compiled and edited by Elizabeth Longford) *Ladies in Waiting; the Personal Diaries and Albums of Louisa,*

Lady in Waiting to Queen Victoria and Queen Alexandra. Mayflower Books, 1979.

Barlow, Glyn. *The Story of Madras.* The Project Gutenberg eBook #26621. 2008. https://www.gutenberg.org/cache/epub/26621/pg26621-images.html

Barnett, Correlli. *Britain and her Army, 1509-1970; a Military, Political and Social Survey.* Morrow, 1970.

Bayley, Emily Clive. The *Golden Calm; an English Lady's Life in Moghul Delhi.* Ed. By M.M. Kaye. Viking, 1980.

Bhat, Mahesh. *Bengaluru/Bangalore; In First Person Singular.* Mahesh Bhat Publishing, 2012.

Blake, William. (1757-1827) *The Tyger.* poets.org/poem/tyger

Blunt, Alison. *Domicile and Diaspora; Anglo-Indian Women and the Spatial Politics of Home.* (RGS-IBG Book Series.) Blackwell Publishing, 2005.

Brennan, Jennifer. *Curries and Bugles; a Memoir and Cookbook of the British Raj.* Viking, 1990. Penguin Books 1992. Republished Periplus Editions. 2000.

Brown, Judith M., and Robert Eric Frykenberg. *Christians, Cultural Interactions, and India's Religious Traditions.* (Studies in the History of Christian Missions series.) Eerdmans Publishing Co, 2002.

Brown, Patricia. *Anglo-Indian Food and Customs.* Penguin Books India, 1998. Tenth Anniversary Edition. iUniverse; Anniversary edition. 2008.

Buehler, George. *Laws of Manu.* Krisna Press. AMS. (BCL ser II Reprint of 1886 ed.)

Caplan, Lionel. *"Colonial and Contemporary Transnationalisms: Traversing Anglo-Indian Boundaries of the Mind."* 2003 http://home.alphalink.com.au/~agilbert/cap0399

Cassity, Kathleen and Rochelle Almeida, editors *Curtain Call: Anglo-Indian Reflections.* CTR Inc. Publishing, 2015.

Chamberlain, Jacob. *The Kingdom in India; its Progress and Its Promise.* With a biographical sketch by Henry Nitchie Cobb. Fleming H. Revell Company, 1908. o.p., reprinted 2015.

Charlton-Stevens, Uther. *Anglo-Indians and Minority Politics in South Asia: Race, Boundary Making and Communal Nationalism* (Royal Asiatic Society) Routledge, 2020.

Collingham, Lizzie. *Curry: a Tale of Cooks and Conquerors.* Oxford University Press, 2006.

Cotta, Joseph. *A Heritage of Indian Cooking.* 3rd edition. Paragon Printers, 1990.

Croker, B. M. *In Old Madras.* Classic Reprint. ForgottenBooks, 2018. (orig. Hutchinson & Co) (Fiction.) Available in pdf from www.forgottenbooks.com

Crossette, Barbara. *The Great Hill Stations of Asia.* Rev. ed. Basic Books, 1998. *"Kodaikanal and Ootacamund"* p.92-119.

Daniel, Ruby, and Barbara C. Johnson. *Ruby of Cochin: An Indian Jewish Woman Remembers.* (Portions from Four Centuries of Jewish Women's Spirituality). The Jewish Publication Society, 1995.

De Coury, Anne *The Fishing Fleet: husband-hunting in the Raj.* HarperCollins Publishers, 2014.

Deefholts, Margaret. *Haunting India: a Collection of Short Fiction,*

Poems, Travel Tales and Memoirs. Calcutta Tiljallah Relief, Inc. (CTR) 2003.

—-. *India: A Travel Writer's Tales.* First Choice Books, 2021.

—-. and Sylvia W. Staub, editors. *Voices on the Verandah: An Anthology of Anglo-Indian Prose and Poetry.* CTR Inc. Publishing, 2004.

—-. and Glenn Deefholts, editors. *The Way We Were: Anglo-Indian Chronicles.* CTR Inc. Publishing, 2006

—-. and Susan Deefholts, editors. *Women of Anglo-India: Tales and Memoirs.* CTR Inc. Publishing, 2010.

Dias, Charles. *The Anglo-Indians and their Future.* (Heritage Study series) Pranatha, 2019.

Dalrymple, William. *The Anarchy: the relentless rise of the East India Company.* Bloomsbury Publishing, 2019.

—-. *White Mughals: Love and Betrayal in Eighteenth Century India.* Viking, 2003.

David, Robert. *A Land I once called Home.* BDB Books, 2005. Designed and printed by Harry MacLure Design Studio.

Edwardes, Michael. *Bound to Exile, the Victorians in India.* Praeger, 1969. ("*The Police-Wallah's Little Dinner*" p. 216). Victorian & Modern History Book Club, London; Book Club edition, 1972.

Edwardes, Michael. *British India 1772-1947: a Survey of the Nature and Effects of Alien Rule.* Taplinger, 1967.

Encyclopedia Britannica. Eleventh Edition. University Press NY. 1910. This edition has extensive texts about India with detailed illustrations. It is now in the public domain and sections of text appear online.

Estibeiro, C. M. *Goa; Yesterday and Today*. Goa, 2002.

Fay, Eliza. *Original Letters from India*. Originally published 1925. E. M. Forster, editor. Introduction by Simon Winchester. New York Review of Books Classics, Reprint edition 2010.

Foley, Tricia. *The Romance of British Colonial Style*. Clarkson Potter, 1993.

Fowler, Marian. *Below the Peacock Fan: First Ladies of the Raj*. Viking, 1987

Friend in Need. *English-Tamil Cookery Book*. Compiled by The Ladies' Committee F.I.N.S (Friend in Need Society) Women's Workshop. 3rd Edition. Madras, 1950. First edition, 1938.

Gabb, Alfred. *Anglo-Indian Legacy*. Second edition. Beryl Pogson Books, 2000.

Gaikwad, V.R. *The Anglo-Indians: A Study in the Problems and Processes Involved in Emotional and Cultural Integration*. Asia Publishing House (Taplinger) 1967. Reprint 2003.

Gantzer, Hugh and Colleen Gantzer. *Lynsdale Ray: a historical novel*. Niyogi Books. 2015.

—-. *Spicestory*. Niyogi Books. 2014. Many other books by this author (husband and wife) team.

Gilbert, Adrian. Editor (original) Online journal since 1996 now morphed into the *International Journal of Anglo-Indian Studies (IJAIS)* http://www.international-journal-of-anglo-indian-studies.org Registration and log in required to submit. Searchable archives. For a list of hyperlinked articles including The Anglo-Indian Wallah 1996-2014 use http://home.alphalink.com.au/~agilbert/indexold.html

Gilmour, David. *The British in India: a Social History of the Raj*. New York: Farrar, Straus, and Giroux. 2018.

Godden, Jon, and Rumer Godden. *Two under the Indian Sun*. MacMillan, Viking Press. 1966.

Grundler, Johann Ernst and Bartholomaus Ziegenbalg *"Die Malabarische Korrespondenz. Tamilische Briefe and deutsche Missionare. Eine Auswahl."* (Foreign Cultures in old reports Bd. 5) Kurt Leiebau, editor. [The Malabar correspondence. *Tamil Letters to German Missionaries, a Selection*] Jan Thorbecke Pub. Co., 1998.

Haslam, Jillian. *Indian. English*. New Generation Publishing, 2011.

Havell, Ernest Binfield. *The History of Aryan Rule in India; from the Earliest Times to the Death of Akbar*. Harrap & Co. approx. 1930. Reprinted 2015 and 2019. Illustrated.

Hawes, Christopher. *Poor Relations; the Making of a Eurasian Community in British India 1773-1883*. Curzon, 1996.

Higham, Charles, and Roy Moseley. *Princess Merle: the Romantic Life of Merle Oberon*. Coward-McCann, 1983.

Hobson-Johson: A Glossary of Colloquial Anglo-Indian Words and Phrases, and of Kindred Terms, Etymological, Historical, Geographical and Discursive. Compiled by Henry Yule and Arthur Coke Burnell in 1886. William Crooke ed. John Murray, 1903. (Another new edition published by Oxford World Classics in 2015.) Available in the searchable database *Digital Dictionaries of South Asia* https://dsalsrv04.uchicago.edu/dictionaries/hobsonjobson/ and Google Books.

Issar, T.P. *The City Beautiful: A Celebration of the Architectural Heritage and City-aesthetics of Bangalore*. Bangalore Urban Art Commission, 1988. (State Bank of India residence on p. 70-71.)

Jolly, Emma. *Tracing Your British Indian Ancestors; A Guide for Family Historians.* Pen & Sword Family History, 2012.

Khajane, Muralidhara. "*Of elegance and heritage, Hopeville comprises a colonial building and annex on a 12-acre area.*" The Hindu, July 2013.

Kaye, M. M. ed. *The Golden Calm: an English Lady's Life in the Moghul Delhi. Reminiscences by Emily, Lady Clive Bayley, and by her father, Sir Thomas Metcalfe.* Viking Press, 1980.

Kendal, Felicity. *White Cargo; A Memoir.* Penguin Books, 1998. Includes her memories of India.

Kennedy, Dane. *The Magic Mountains: Hill Stations and the British Raj.* University of California Press, 1996.

Kipling, Rudyard. *Rudyard Kipling's Verse: definitive Edition.* Doubleday & Company, 1940.

Kuruvita, Peter. *Serendip; My Sri Lankan Kitchen.* Murdoch Books, 2009.

Lewis, Jared Robin. *E. M. Forster's Passages to India.* Columbia University Press, 1979.

Love, Henry Davison. *Vestiges of Old Madras, 1640-1800; traced from the East India Company's Records preserved at Fort St. George and the India Office, and from other sources.* Vol. 4. Index Volume. (India Records Series) John Murray, 1913.

Lumb, Lionel, editor. *More Voices on the Verandah; an Anglo-Indian Anthology.* CTR Inc. Publishing, 2012.

—-. and Deborah Van Veldhuizen, editors. *The Way We Are: An Anglo-Indian Mosaic.* CTR Inc. Publishing, 2008. Some chapters available on

Google Books https://www.google.com/books/edition/
The_Way_We_Are/pP_TdfyFDQEC?hl=en&gbpv=1&kptab

Lyons, Esther Mary. *Bittersweet Truth; Recollections of an Anglo-Indian Born During the Last Years of the British Raj.* D.K. Publishers Distributors. 2001.

Macaulay, Thomas Babington. *Macaulay's Essay on Warren Hastings.* Samuel M. Tucker, editor. Longmans, Green and Co. 1910. (1841) o.p. Available on http://www.columbia.edu/itc/mealac/pritchett/00generallinks/macaulay/hastings/txt_complete.html

The Madras Almanac 1825, Fort St. George lists the Civil, Judicial, and Medical establishments and of the Europeans not in the King's or Company's service. Published for the benefit of the military male orphan asylum. Asylum Press. o. p.

Map of the Madras Presidency; Showing the Roads and Distances. Central Survey Office, 1926.

Marks, Copeland. *The Varied Kitchens of India; cuisines of the Anglo-Indians of Calcutta, Bengalis, Jews of Calcutta, Kashmiris, Parsis and Tibetans of Darjeeling.* M. Evans & Company, 1986.

Moore, Gloria Jean. *The Anglo-Indian Vision.* AE Press, 1986

Moorhouse, Geoffrey. *India Britannica.* HarperCollins, 1983.

—-. *The Missionaries.* Lippincott, 1973. Readers Union Edition, 1975.

Moss, Peter (MBE). *Bye Bye Blackbird; an Anglo-Indian Memoir.* iUniverse, 2004.

"We need fresh voices and fresh perspectives,"
—Peter Moss, MBE (1935-2019).

Peter encouraged me to write about the Anglo-Indian life we had in common.

Muttha, Suttha. *"It once housed the Resident"* (Hopeville). *Namma Bangalore - Mysore: The cities that never cease to surprise* (blog) September 15, 2013. http://ramubangalore.blogspot.com/2013/09/it-once-housed-resident.html

Muthiah, S. *Madras that is Chennai: Gateway to the South.* Ranpar Publishers, 2005.

—-. and Harry MacLure. *The Anglo-Indians; a 500-Year History.* Niyogi Books, 2017.

Nehra, Arvind. *Letters of an Indian Judge to an English Gentlewoman.* Peter Davies, 1934. Reprinted 1971.

Nicolson, Nigel. *Mary Curzon.* Harper & Row, 1977.

Noble, Arthur H. *The Chase Family.* Heraldry Today, 1967.

Old and New British Recipes; to aid British War Relief, 1940. Compiled by Adelaide M. Owen. British War Relief Association of Northern California, 1940.

Oliver, Charles. *Dinner at Buckingham Palace.* Prentice-Hall, 1972 Republished John Blake, 2019.

A memoir is a seminal work. "These are what we researchers rely on as primary sources."
—Brent H. Otto, SJ. Author of the dissertation *Anglo-Indians in the Tumultuous Years: Community, Nationalism, War and Emigration*, 1939-1955.

Panter-Downes, Mollie. *Ooty Preserved, a Victorian Hill Station in India.* Farrar, Straus & Giroux, 1967.

Peppin, Bryan. *Black and White; The 'Anglo-Indian' Identity in Recent English Fiction.* Author House, 2012.

Phillips, Sir Percival. *The Prince of Wales' Eastern Book: A Pictorial Record of the Voyages of H.M.S. 'Renown' 1921-1922.* Hodder and Stoughton, Limited. 1922. o.p.

Price, Frederick. *Ootacamund; a history.* First published 1908. Rupa & Co, 2002.

Rasmussen, Peter Ravn. *Tranquebar, the Danish East Indian Company 1616 - 1669: a brief essay, chiefly in narrative form.* Rev. and Reworked from University of Copenhagen. 1996.

Russell-Wood, A. J. R. *The Portuguese Empire, 1415-1808: A World on the Move.* Second edition. JHUP. 1998.

Salisbury, Charlotte Y. *Tibetan Diary:; and Travels along the Old Silk Route.* Walker & Co, 1981.

Shulman, David Dean. *Tamil Temple Myths: Sacrifice and Divine Marriage in the South Indian Saiva Tradition.* (Princeton Legacy Library) Princeton University Press, 1980.

Solomon, Charmaine. *The Complete Asian Cookbook.* Summit Books, 1976. (McGraw-Hill) Deborah and Nina Solomon, contributors. Hardie Grant, new edition, 2017.

—-. and Reuben Solomon. *The Curry Cookbook.* Lansdowne Press, 1980.

—-. *Love and a Wooden Spoon: Recipes, Anecdotes and Poems to Bring Happiness to the Heart of Young and Old.* Illustrated by Dee Huxley. Hill of Content, 1981. Rev.1992.

Steel, Flora Annie, and Grace Gardiner. *The Complete Indian*

Housekeeper and Cook: Giving Duties of Mistress and Servants the General Management of the House and Practical Recipes for Cooking in all its Branches. 1st ed, 1898. New Ed. 1901. New and Rev. Ed. 1904 Reprinted, Read Books Ltd. 2020.

Stracey, Eric. *Growing up in Anglo India.* East West Books, 2000.

Thompson, Carrie. *Carrie Thompson's Mem Saheb's Cookery.* Vest & Co, 1908. o.p.

Trollope, Joanna. *Britannia's Daughters: Women of the British Empire.* International ed. Pimlico, 2006.

Tuan, Yi-Fu. *Space and Place; the Perspective of Experience.* University of Minnesota Press, 1977. "Attachment to Homeland" Chapter 11 p. 149-160.

University of Calcutta. University Library. *Anglo Indian Collection.* (No hyphen) Search the Online Catalog within the Anglo-Indian Collection. https://www.caluniv.ac.in/opac/

Veerasawmy, E. P. *Indian Cookery; for use in all countries.* Jaico, 1956. (Arco Pub. 1953) Reprints Pendragon and Amazon.com.

Von Welanetz, Diana and Paul Von Welanetz. *The Von Welanetz Guide to Ethnic Ingredients:; How to buy and prepare more than 1000 foods from around the world.* J. P. Tarcher, 1982. Grand Central Pub Paperback edition, 1987.

Wheeler, J. Talboys. *Madras in the Olden Time; Being a History of the Presidency from the First Foundation of Fort St. George to the Occupation of Madras by the French 1639-1748.* Compiled from Official Records. Higginbotham and Co. 1882. Google Books https://www.google.com/books/edition/Madras_in_the_Olden_Time/eONAAQAAMAAJ?hl=en&gbpv=1&dq=Madras+in+Golden+Time&pg=PA5&printsec=frontcover

White-Kumar, Bridget *Anglo-Indian Recipes* http://anglo-indianrecipes. blogspot.com/ *Anglo-Indian Cuisine; a legacy of Flavors from the Past, Authentic Anglo-Indian Recipes* and *A Collection of Simple Anglo-Indian Recipes.* Author House, 2013 and other books by Bridget White (Kumar).

Wikipedia. http://www.wikipedia.com This has become a useful resource, with caution because of its open editing policy, allowing any one to edit, use or post information.

Wilbur, Marguerite Eyer. *The East India Company and the British Empire in the Far East.* Stanford University Press, 1945.

Williams, Blair R. *Anglo-Indians Vanishing Remnants of a Bygone Era: Anglo-Indians in India, North America and the UK in 2000.* CTR Books. (Harry MacLure Design Studio, Madras) 2002.

Wilson, Dorothy Clarke. *Dr. Ida; the Torch of Life.* Vellore Christian Medical College Board (USA), Inc. 1976. Copyright, 1959.

Worswick, Clark and Ainslie Embree. *The Last Empire; Photography in British India, 1855-1911.* Aperture, 1976. Reprinted 2005.

Young, Desmond. *Fountain of the Elephants.* Harper, 1959. (Biography of Benoit de Boigne, a soldier of fortune set in 18th Century India.)

29

PUBLISHED WORKS
OF JOY CHASE

Chase, Joy. "*A Christian High School in India*" in Moody Monthly. May 1959. Vol. 59 no. 9 p. 63

——. "*A Great Escape*" South Bay Accent Magazine (Books) Jun/July 1988 p 18-19

——. "*All Wrapped Up*" South Bay Accent Magazine (Books) December/January 1988

——. "*And the Envelope Please…*" South Bay Accent Magazine. December/January 1986/87. p.30+.

——. "*Automated Housing*" High Technology Careers Magazine (Lifestyle Column). June/July 1991.

——. "*Breaking into Regionals*" Writer's Connection February 1988 p 8-9.11

——. "*Collecting Classic Antiques*" South Bay Accent Magazine. (Dollars and Cents) October/November 1988 p. 24-25.

—-. *"Cotton Mary; a review"* INDIA_L Archives, May 27, 2000. 0959459481.

—-. *"Decorating in Style"* South Bay Accent Magazine. (Books) April/May 1988 p.18-19

—-. *"Do you need a Psychic?"* Local Color Autumn 1986. Vol. 3 No. 3, p. 33+ (about Sylvia Browne.)

—-. *"Femme Feng Shui"* in *Women of Anglo-India; Tales and Memories.* Edited by Margaret Deefholts and Susan Deefholts. CTR Inc. 2010. p. 104-107.

—-. *"Five Flags"* in *The Way We Are: an Anglo-Indian Mosaic.* Edited by Lionel Lumb and Deborah Van Veldhuizen. CTR Inc. 2008. p. 186-192.

—-. *"The Information Search: Libraries and Other Sources"* in *Thresholds: Literature-Based Composition.* Harcourt Brace College Publishers, 1995.

—-. *"Jazzing Up Your Summer Wardrobe"* South Bay Accent Magazine June/July 1987 p 22, 25.

—-. *"Library Offerings for Young Adults."* Pacifica Coastside Chronicle. Millbrae/Burlingame Recorder-Progress. San Bruno Herald. South San Francisco Enterprise Journal. Saturday. May 14, 1983. p. 8.

—-. *"Local Designers: Holiday and Cruise Wear."* Local Color Winter 1985. Vol. 2 No. 4.

—-. *"Memories of the Raj; a poem"* in *Leaf by Leaf.* Evergreen Valley College. Spring 2006 p. 102.

—-. *"Rich Flavor of the Raj; Anglo-Indian culture is more than a movie."*

San Jose Mercury News. March 20, 1985. Section E, cover story. Recipes, p. 2E.

—. *"Selecting Antiques"* South Bay Accent Magazine (Dollars & Cents) October/November 1988 Vol. 11 No. 2 p 24.

—. *"Selecting a School; a parent's dilemma."* Local Color Spring 1986. Vol. 3 No. 1, p. 35+.

—. *"Sikhs in America; a book review."* India Currents February 1992. p.M6.

—. *"Spine Tinglers"* South Bay Accent Magazine (Books). August/September 1988 Vol. 11 p. 18-19.

—. *"Stars; a poem."* in *Leaf by Leaf:* Evergreen Valley College. Pearson Publishing. Spring 1999 p.37

—. *"South Bay Style."* South Bay Accent Magazine. August/September 1986. Vol. 9 No. 1, p. 28-29.

—. *"The Psychics Predict"* South Bay Accent Magazine December/January 1988

—. *"The Research Paper. Information Search: Libraries and Other Sources"* In *Instructor's Manual to accompany Thresholds Literature-Based Composition,* by J. Sterling Warner (Evergreen Valley College) Part III: Materials and Methods of Modern Research (Chapters 16-17) p. 139-141. Harcourt Brace College Publishers 1996.

—. *"Take the Dream Town Train"* South Bay Accent Magazine (Books) February/March 1988

—. *"Twenty Children; 25 Years Later."* Local Color Spring 1986. Vol. 3 No. 1, p.33+

—-. *Turning Work into Fun*. South Bay Accent Magazine. (Books) October/November 1988. P. 20-21

Chase, Joy, and Carol Kaczmark. *"Books for Adults: Young People."* Wisconsin Library Bulletin. May-June 1970. Vol. 66 No. 3, p. 179-183.

Chase, Joy, Wiley Hampton, and Virginia Ross. *"East Palo Alto Library Services Project—San Mateo County Library."* in Newsnotes of California Libraries; Official Journal of the California State Library. Summer 1972. Vol. 67 No. 3, p. 347-353.

MORE ABOUT THE AUTHOR

I came to America alone at the age of twenty-two with twenty U.S. dollars and two British pounds in my handbag. My lack of cash did not bother me much at that age. I was mostly concerned with the high heel sandals that I wore for the entire flights. In fact, they broke down by the time I reached London. Luckily, my friend from high school, Elspeth, worked in the shoe department of Harrod's Department Store at the time. I met her there and told her about my lose heel. She asked me to take it off and proceeded to hammer it together on the swanky wooden floor of Harrods. I was shocked! After all, I had heard that the Queen shopped at Harrods in those days. I expected to see her around every corner.

I had taken the train from Madras to Bombay with my mother and we met my dad who was there on business. My flight on a Viscount aircraft stopped at several airports enroute. In Bagdad, we were delayed for four hours because of a hydraulic leak on the plane. When we re-boarded, I accidently left the U. S. required X-ray of my lungs in the bathroom and the plane was held up until it was back in my hands. At that time, people traveling from India to the United States had to carry with them a current X-ray of their lungs to prove they did not have tuberculosis. I carried mine. Now we have to prove we are clear of the novel coronavirus.

Next, we stopped in Beirut. Both Iraq and Lebanon would later be gutted by wars. I looked out at the beautiful horizon and saw trees in the distance that I learned were cedars—the biblical cedars of Lebanon. On to Zurich, where I bought an umbrella folded into an immaculately sewn leather sheath with my meager money. Then to London where I spent a week with friends of my parents and some friends of mine. I cannot say I was scared to be traveling alone on this pioneering journey. I was curious, excited, and a little nervous. I had not yet learned the monotone accent of the Midwest and spoke with a lilt I had learned in the British boarding school I had attended before college. This sometimes led to questions about my origins which felt invasive and personal.

I arrived in New York in the summer, but I did not see New York City until many years later. I was keenly observant and felt a longing to be with young people around my age. When I finally arrived in Minneapolis in Minnesota, I attended a short orientation before joining Bethel College in St. Paul for the fall. Two months after I started school, John F. Kennedy, the President of the United States was shot and killed.

It was an epic journey, but I yearned for India, the place of my birth and my childhood. I could never forget and I often reminiscence, longing for the earthy goodness and the heady assault to the senses of the cities, towns, and villages of India.

I went to elementary and high school mostly in Madras and in the Nilgiris. When I graduated from high school, I spent a year studying shorthand and typing in Cochin because my school principal suggested to my parents that I could get a good job as a secretary. I vowed to myself that I would never be anyone's secretary. I wanted to do the job and not help someone else to do it. My parents secretly hoped I would get married first and foremost. My mother told me that she had prayed until the last day that I would find a man to accompany me to America. Alas, I did not, but maybe that was a good thing.

I had been admitted to Queen Mary's College, in the University of Madras in India and got my bachelor's degree mostly studying Shakespeare, Milton and the Social History of England. It was totally out of context with the country I lived in. Nevertheless, I loved Shakespeare and had read most of his plays before I went to college. I took a correspondence class in journalism from the London School of Journalism while at college in Madras.

I did one year of literature at Bethel College in St. Paul studying World and American Literature. I was accepted to the University of Wisconsin-Madison into the School of Library and Information Science where I received my master's degree. I joined the workforce as a librarian and I'm still a librarian.

My passport photo, 1963

I married William Menezes who was from Ethiopia although his parents had migrated from Goa. I took some time out from working when our children, Natala and Sheila, were born and spent some years at home raising them before getting divorced and returning to work at two community college libraries in San Jose, California. Although officially retired, I still work there part-time as an adjunct associate. I live in the San Francisco Bay Area now. I wish I could beam up to India now and then.

My daughters R-L Natala and Sheila in 2019

I think I have come of age but when did I have my coming-of-age ceremony? When I turned twenty-one in India, I asked my mother to give me a ruby ring that she had, and she did. Unfortunately, a few years later it was one of the pieces of precious jewelry that was stolen from my house in Mountain View. There was no ceremony when I turned twenty-one and I don't remember a party or anything special about it, except to me. I was probably away at college in Madras. Later, I came to America when I was twenty-two and that may have been my coming out, but I was so tenuous and trying to learn the culture and country on warp speed that I don't think I was aware enough of myself to say that I really came out. Then there were my graduations, my marriages, the birth of my daughters, my re-entering the workforce, my retirement. Not rituals but some of them had ceremonies. Now that I have turned eighty, I feel that I have come of age, and I don't need any ceremony or ritual. I turned eighty during the pandemic lockdown and we could not have a party, but my daughters helped me to celebrate, and my friends and family sent me video messages that were delightful. Here I am alone but not lonely, journeying towards the end of my life. Maybe I'll live to be one hundred like my mother. Maybe I will die tonight.

> No one knows when their hour will come; as fish are caught in a cruel net, or birds are taken in a snare, so people are trapped by evil times that fall unexpectedly upon them.
>
> — ECCLESIASTES 9:12 (NIV)

Taken near my home in Redwood City with my dog, Brizzy.

When I dream then I'm in India. The warm tropical afternoons beckon. Still and balmy they invite sleep. I'm back on a cool verandah, the ocean waves rhythmically whooshing back and forth. Maybe under a shack covered in coconut sheaves blocking the sharp sun's glare from my eyes. I dream of big rooms and brightly colored flower gardens where butterflies and dragonflies abound. Sometimes I run and run, free as a child searching for something I never find. I awake and know that I am home.

Stars
Dedicated to Anglo-Indians everywhere

You put the stars into my eyes
Shining in the night.
You make me sing around the house
Little lies and laughter.
You and I together in this place
Fill our world with joy.
Who cares of the stock market crash,
The sun will come up for us.
Soak in a tub filled with praises,
Recording on silly devices,
Remembered past times of sadness
Makes us feel dull and bored.
Today is a refuge—the future too far,
Money so mundane but needed.
Sweetness to share what is now,
A bag full of quarters will do.
Willing to throw diamonds down—
A moonlit night is enough,
To share the history of us.

Published in Leaf by Leaf (literary journal) Evergreen Valley College, Pearson Custom Publishing, Spring, 1999.